Chapter 1: Introduction to Assembly Language

Section 1.1: What is Assembly Language?

Assembly language is a low-level programming language that is closely tied to a computer's architecture. Unlike high-level programming languages like Python, C++, or Java, which are designed to be human-readable and easy to write, assembly language is a symbolic representation of machine code instructions. Each assembly language instruction corresponds to a single machine-level instruction that can be executed directly by the computer's central processing unit (CPU).

Assembly language provides a way for programmers to interact with a computer's hardware at a fundamental level. It allows programmers to write code that is specific to a particular CPU architecture, making it highly efficient and giving them precise control over the computer's resources. Assembly language is often used for tasks where performance is critical, such as writing device drivers, real-time systems, and embedded systems programming.

Assembly Language Mnemonics

In assembly language, instructions are represented using mnemonics, which are short, easy-to-remember codes that correspond to specific operations. For example, the mnemonic MOV is often used to represent a data movement operation, such as copying a value from one memory location to another. Each mnemonic is associated with a specific operation code (opcode) that the CPU understands.

Here's a simple example of assembly code that adds two numbers and stores the result in a register:

```
MOV AX, 5      ; Load the value 5 into register AX
MOV BX, 3      ; Load the value 3 into register BX
ADD AX, BX     ; Add the values in AX and BX, result in AX
```

In this code, MOV is used to move values into registers, and ADD is used to perform addition. Assembly language instructions are highly specific to the CPU architecture being used, so the above code might work on one type of CPU but not on another.

Registers and Memory

Assembly language programs primarily work with two types of storage: registers and memory. Registers are small, fast storage locations within the CPU itself, and they are used for temporary data storage and manipulation. Memory, on the other hand, is external storage that holds both program instructions and data.

Registers play a crucial role in assembly language programming because they can be accessed much faster than memory. Assembly instructions often involve moving data between registers and memory, performing operations on register contents, and storing the results back in registers or memory.

Assembly Language Programming Paradigm

Assembly language programming is often described as a low-level and imperative programming paradigm. It is considered low-level because it operates closely with the hardware and is specific to a particular CPU architecture. It is imperative because programmers write a sequence of instructions that explicitly specify the steps the computer should take to perform a task.

In contrast to high-level languages, which use more abstract and expressive constructs like functions, loops, and conditional statements, assembly language requires programmers to have a deep understanding of the CPU's architecture and its instruction set.

Conclusion

Assembly language serves as a bridge between human-readable code and the machine-level instructions that a computer's CPU can execute. While it requires a greater level of expertise and knowledge of a computer's architecture, it provides unparalleled control and performance for certain types of programming tasks. As we delve deeper into this book, we will explore the historical perspective of assembly, its benefits and challenges, and how to set up your assembly development environment.

Section 1.2: Historical Perspective of Assembly

The history of assembly language is closely intertwined with the development of computers themselves. In this section, we will take a journey through time to explore the historical perspective of assembly language and how it has evolved over the years.

Early Assembly Languages

The concept of assembly language emerged in the early days of computing when computers were large and operated with vacuum tubes and punched cards. Programmers initially wrote machine code directly, which was a tedious and error-prone process. To simplify programming, assembly languages were introduced.

Assembly languages in the early days were specific to each computer model or architecture. Programmers had to learn a unique assembly language for each computer they worked on, making it a challenging and specialized skill.

The Birth of High-Level Languages

As computing technology advanced, the need for higher-level abstractions became evident. High-level programming languages like Fortran and COBOL were developed to provide a more human-readable and portable way of writing code. These languages allowed programmers to write code without needing in-depth knowledge of the computer's hardware.

However, even as high-level languages gained popularity, assembly language retained its significance. Programmers often needed to write critical sections of code in assembly to optimize performance or access hardware directly.

Assembly Language in the Era of Microprocessors

The introduction of microprocessors in the 1970s revolutionized computing. These small, affordable CPUs made computers accessible to a broader audience. As microprocessors became more prevalent, assembly languages were adapted to work with these new processors.

Assembly languages for microprocessors like the Intel 8080 and Motorola 6800 were developed, and they played a crucial role in the early days of personal computing. Assembly allowed programmers to write software that ran efficiently on these early microcomputers.

The Rise of High-Level Languages and Compilers

With the proliferation of microprocessors and personal computers, high-level programming languages gained dominance. Languages like C, C++, and later, Python and Java, became popular choices for software development. Compilers and interpreters translated high-level code into machine code, eliminating the need for programmers to write assembly language for most applications.

While assembly language continued to be used in certain areas, such as system programming and embedded systems, its prominence in mainstream software development diminished.

Assembly Language in the Modern Era

In the modern era, assembly language remains relevant in specific domains. It is commonly used in tasks that require low-level control over hardware, such as writing device drivers, operating systems, and firmware for embedded systems. Additionally, assembly language is valuable in optimizing critical code sections in performance-critical applications.

In recent years, there has been renewed interest in assembly language for specialized computing platforms, such as graphics programming for GPUs and low-level code for IoT devices.

Conclusion

The historical perspective of assembly language reflects its evolution from the early days of computing to its continued relevance in specific niches of the modern computing landscape. While high-level languages dominate general-purpose programming, assembly language remains a powerful tool for those who require fine-grained control over hardware and performance optimization. In the following sections, we will explore the benefits and challenges of working with assembly language and its comparison to high-level languages.

Section 1.3: Benefits and Challenges of Assembly

Assembly language programming offers a unique set of advantages and presents specific challenges to programmers. In this section, we will delve into the benefits and challenges associated with working in assembly language.

Benefits of Assembly Language

1. **Efficiency:** Assembly language provides fine-grained control over a computer's hardware, allowing programmers to write highly optimized code. This level of control can result in more efficient and faster-running programs, making it suitable for performance-critical tasks.

2. **Direct Hardware Access:** Assembly language allows direct access to a computer's hardware, including registers, memory, and I/O ports. This is essential for tasks like writing device drivers and interfacing with specialized hardware.

3. **Portability:** While assembly language is specific to a particular CPU architecture, it can still be somewhat portable within that architecture family. Code can often be adapted to run on different CPUs within the same family with minimal modifications.

4. **Low-Level Debugging:** Assembly language offers insights into the inner workings of a program and can be valuable for debugging at the lowest level. Programmers can trace instructions step by step and analyze memory contents in detail.

5. **Size Control:** Assembly programs can be extremely compact, which is beneficial in environments with limited memory, such as embedded systems or firmware.

Challenges of Assembly Language

1. **Steep Learning Curve:** Assembly language is known for its complexity and requires a deep understanding of CPU architecture. Learning and mastering assembly can be time-consuming and challenging, especially for newcomers to programming.

2. **Platform-Specific:** Assembly code is highly specific to a particular CPU architecture, making it non-portable between different processor families. Code written for one architecture may need significant modifications to run on another.

3. **Error-Prone:** Assembly code is prone to human errors, and debugging can be challenging, especially for complex programs. A single mistake can lead to hard-to-trace bugs.

4. **Limited Expressiveness:** Assembly lacks the high-level constructs and abstractions found in languages like C++ or Python. Writing complex algorithms in assembly can be laborious and error-prone.

5. **Maintenance Difficulty:** Maintaining and modifying assembly code can be challenging, as changes in hardware or requirements may necessitate significant code revisions. This can lead to increased development time and costs.

6. **Reduced Development Productivity:** Writing programs in assembly often takes longer compared to high-level languages. This can be a significant drawback in time-sensitive projects.

7. **Decreased Code Readability:** Assembly code can be cryptic and challenging to understand, which makes it less accessible to other programmers and hinders collaboration.

In summary, assembly language offers unparalleled control and efficiency but comes with a steep learning curve, platform-specificity, and increased complexity. It is a tool best suited for specialized applications where performance and hardware interaction are paramount, rather than general-purpose software development. In the subsequent sections, we will explore the differences between assembly language and high-level languages and guide you in setting up your assembly development environment.

Section 1.4: Assembly Language vs. High-Level Languages

In the world of programming, developers have a choice between using assembly language and high-level languages like Python, C++, or Java. Each option has its strengths and weaknesses, and the choice between them depends on the specific requirements of a project. In this section, we will compare assembly language and high-level languages to highlight their differences and help you understand when to use each.

Expressiveness

High-level languages are designed with the goal of providing a high level of abstraction. They offer a rich set of built-in data types, control structures, and libraries that make it easier for programmers to express complex algorithms and ideas in a concise and readable manner. This expressiveness is a significant advantage when developing large-scale applications, algorithms, or systems.

Assembly language, on the other hand, is inherently less expressive. It lacks the high-level constructs found in languages like C++ or Python, which means that programmers must often write more lines of code to accomplish the same task. This can make assembly less suitable for projects that require rapid development and code readability.

Efficiency

Assembly language is known for its efficiency. Programs written in assembly can be highly optimized because they allow programmers to take full advantage of a computer's hardware resources. Assembly code can be tailored to specific CPU architectures and can achieve the best possible performance.

High-level languages prioritize developer productivity and portability over low-level optimization. While compilers and interpreters can generate efficient code, they may not be able to match the level of optimization achieved by handcrafted assembly code. For tasks where performance is critical, such as real-time systems or device drivers, assembly language is often the preferred choice.

Portability

High-level languages are designed to be portable across different platforms and architectures. Code written in a high-level language can be compiled or interpreted for various operating systems and CPU architectures with minimal modifications. This portability simplifies the development process and allows developers to target a broader range of hardware.

Assembly language, in contrast, is highly platform-specific. Code written for one CPU architecture may not run on another without significant modifications. Porting assembly code to different architectures is a complex and time-consuming process, making it less suitable for projects that require cross-platform compatibility.

Development Speed

High-level languages are favored for their rapid development capabilities. Programmers can write, test, and debug code more quickly in high-level languages due to their built-in abstractions and easy-to-understand syntax. This speed of development is essential for projects with tight deadlines or rapidly evolving requirements.

Assembly language, while powerful, tends to be slower in terms of development. Writing and debugging assembly code is a more meticulous and time-consuming process. For projects where time-to-market is critical, high-level languages provide a significant advantage.

Maintenance and Readability

High-level languages generally result in more maintainable and readable code. Their syntax is designed to be human-friendly, making it easier for multiple developers to collaborate on a project. Additionally, high-level languages often include features like functions, classes, and libraries that promote code modularity and reusability.

Assembly language, with its low-level nature, can lead to less readable and more error-prone code. Programs written in assembly may require more extensive documentation and comments to make the code understandable to others. This can increase the effort required for code maintenance and updates.

Conclusion

In summary, the choice between assembly language and high-level languages depends on the specific needs of a project. High-level languages excel in terms of expressiveness, development speed, portability, and code readability, making them a solid choice for most software development tasks. Assembly language, on the other hand, shines when it comes to efficiency and fine-grained hardware control, making it valuable for performance-critical applications, embedded systems, and low-level system programming.

As we progress through this book, you'll gain a deeper understanding of assembly language and how to leverage its strengths for various purposes, while also recognizing the advantages of high-level languages in different scenarios.

Section 1.5: Setting Up Your Assembly Development Environment

Setting up an assembly language development environment is a crucial first step in your journey to becoming proficient in assembly programming. In this section, we will guide you through the process of setting up the tools and resources you need to start writing and testing assembly code.

Choose an Assembly Language

Before setting up your development environment, it's essential to decide which assembly language you'll be working with. Assembly languages are specific to different CPU architectures, so your choice will depend on the target platform or CPU you plan to program for. Common assembly languages include x86, ARM, MIPS, and many others.

Install a Text Editor or Integrated Development Environment (IDE)

To write assembly code, you need a text editor or an integrated development environment (IDE). Some popular choices for writing assembly code include:

- **Visual Studio Code (VSCode):** VSCode is a versatile code editor with extensions available for various assembly languages.

- **Notepad++:** Notepad++ is a lightweight text editor with syntax highlighting support for assembly languages.

- **Eclipse:** If you prefer an integrated development environment, Eclipse can be configured for assembly development with suitable plugins.

Choose the one that best suits your preferences and workflow.

Assembler and Compiler

You'll need an assembler and, in some cases, a compiler to convert your assembly code into machine code or object code. The specific tools you need depend on the assembly language you've chosen. For example, for x86 assembly, you can use the NASM (Netwide Assembler) as your assembler.

Debugging Tools

Debugging is an essential part of assembly language programming. You'll need debugging tools to help you find and fix issues in your code. GDB (GNU Debugger) is a widely used debugger that supports assembly language debugging for various architectures.

Emulators and Simulators

If you don't have access to the actual hardware you're targeting, emulators or simulators can be invaluable for testing and debugging. For example, QEMU is a versatile emulator that supports a wide range of CPU architectures and can be used for testing assembly code.

Documentation and Resources

Assembly languages often have extensive documentation available online or in books. Look for official documentation from the CPU manufacturer or community resources that provide tutorials and guides. Having a reliable reference is crucial as you learn and work with assembly.

Configure Your Build Environment

Once you've chosen your tools and resources, you'll need to configure your build environment. This typically involves setting up the paths to your assembler, compiler, and debugger in your development environment. Make sure to follow the documentation and guides for your chosen tools to ensure correct configuration.

Writing Your First Assembly Program

With your development environment set up, you can now start writing your first assembly program. Create a simple program that demonstrates basic assembly language concepts, such as data movement and arithmetic operations. As you write and test your code, refer to your chosen assembly language's syntax and documentation for guidance.

Conclusion

Setting up an assembly language development environment can seem daunting at first, but with the right tools, documentation, and resources, you'll be well-prepared to start your journey into the world of assembly programming. In the subsequent chapters, we will dive deeper into assembly language basics, instruction sets, and practical examples to help you build your skills and confidence as an assembly programmer.

Chapter 2: Assembly Language Basics

Section 2.1: Registers and Memory

In assembly language programming, understanding how data is stored and manipulated is fundamental. This section introduces you to two primary components: registers and memory. These are the building blocks of assembly programming.

Registers

Registers are small, high-speed storage locations within the central processing unit (CPU). Think of them as tiny workspaces where the CPU can perform operations. Registers come in various sizes, typically 8, 16, 32, or 64 bits, depending on the CPU architecture. Commonly used registers include:

- **General-Purpose Registers:** These registers are versatile and can be used for various purposes. In x86 architecture, examples include EAX, EBX, ECX, and EDX.

- **Segment Registers:** These registers are used to manage memory segmentation in older x86 architectures. Examples include CS (Code Segment) and DS (Data Segment).

- **Special-Purpose Registers:** These registers have specific roles, such as EFLAGS (status flags), EIP (instruction pointer), and ESP (stack pointer).

Registers are essential for temporary data storage, calculations, and control flow. They can be accessed very quickly compared to memory, making them crucial for optimizing performance.

Memory

Memory, often referred to as RAM (Random Access Memory), is a more extensive storage space for data and instructions. Memory is organized into individual bytes, each with a unique address. In assembly language, you can access memory by specifying the memory address where data is stored or retrieved.

Memory is where your program's code and data reside. Instructions are fetched from memory and executed, and data is read from or written to memory as needed. Memory access is slower than register access but offers significantly more storage capacity.

Data Movement between Registers and Memory

One of the essential tasks in assembly programming is moving data between registers and memory. You can use specific assembly instructions to perform these operations. For example, the MOV instruction is commonly used to transfer data between a register and memory location:

```
MOV EAX, [MemoryAddress]     ; Load data from MemoryAddress into EAX
MOV [MemoryAddress], EBX     ; Store the value in EBX to MemoryAddress
```

In the first line, data is loaded from a memory location specified by MemoryAddress into the EAX register. In the second line, the value in the EBX register is stored into the memory location MemoryAddress.

Working with Data Sizes

Registers and memory locations have different sizes in terms of bits. When moving data between them, you must consider the size of the data. For example, if you want to load a 32-bit value from memory into a 64-bit register, you need to make sure that the upper bits of the register are properly cleared or preserved.

```
MOV EAX, [MemoryAddress]     ; Load a 32-bit value into EAX
MOVZX RAX, AX                ; Clear upper 32 bits of RAX while preserving lowe
r 32 bits
```

Here, the MOVZX instruction is used to clear the upper 32 bits of the 64-bit RAX register while preserving the lower 32 bits. This ensures that the operation does not leave any unintended data in the upper bits.

Conclusion

Registers and memory are the core elements in assembly language programming. Registers provide high-speed data storage for the CPU, while memory offers larger but comparatively slower storage. Understanding how to move data between registers and memory is crucial for writing effective assembly programs. As you delve deeper into assembly programming, you'll discover how these elements work together to perform complex computations and manipulate data efficiently.

Section 2.2: Data Types and Constants

In assembly language programming, data types and constants play a vital role in defining the nature of data and providing a way to work with it effectively. While assembly languages are low-level and do not have the complex data types of high-level languages, they still have mechanisms for handling various data types and constants.

Data Types

Assembly languages typically support a limited set of fundamental data types:

1. **Byte (8 bits):** The smallest addressable unit of memory. It can represent values from 0 to 255.

2. **Word (16 bits):** A 16-bit data type that can store values from 0 to 65,535.

3. **Doubleword (32 bits):** A 32-bit data type capable of storing values from 0 to 4,294,967,295.

4. **Quadword (64 bits):** A 64-bit data type that can represent values from 0 to 18,446,744,073,709,551,615.

These data types are essential for specifying the size and nature of data when declaring variables or working with memory. The choice of data type affects how much memory is allocated and how operations are performed on that data.

Declaring Constants

Constants are fixed values that do not change during the execution of a program. They are typically used to represent numeric values, addresses, or other data that remains constant throughout the program's execution.

In assembly language, you can declare constants using various methods. One common way is to use the EQU (equals) directive:

```
MY_CONSTANT EQU 42
```

In this example, MY_CONSTANT is defined as the constant value 42. You can use this constant in your program, and its value will be substituted wherever it's referenced.

Initializing Data

When working with data in assembly, you often need to initialize variables or memory locations with specific values. You can use assembly instructions to load values into registers or memory. For instance, to initialize a register with a value, you can use the MOV instruction:

```
MOV EAX, 10   ; Load the value 10 into EAX register
```

To initialize a memory location with a value, you can use similar instructions:

```
MOV [MemoryAddress], 100 ; Store the value 100 at MemoryAddress
```

Memory Allocation

In assembly programming, you may need to allocate memory dynamically during runtime to store data structures or arrays. The specific mechanisms for memory allocation can vary depending on the assembly language and the system's architecture.

Some assembly languages provide system calls or functions for memory allocation, while others require more manual memory management. Understanding memory allocation is crucial for working with data structures efficiently.

String Data

Strings, which are sequences of characters, are commonly used in assembly programming. In many assembly languages, strings are represented as arrays of bytes, with each byte holding a character's ASCII code.

Here's an example of declaring and initializing a string in assembly:

```
MY_STRING DB 'Hello, Assembly!',0   ; Null-terminated string
```

In this example, DB is used to declare a byte, and the string is null-terminated with a null character (0) to indicate its end.

Conclusion

Data types and constants are essential elements of assembly language programming. They help define the nature and size of data, allow you to declare fixed values, and provide a foundation for working with variables and memory. As you progress in your assembly programming journey, you'll become more adept at manipulating different data types and constants to perform a wide range of tasks, from simple arithmetic operations to complex data processing.

Section 2.3: Instruction Set Architecture (ISA)

The Instruction Set Architecture (ISA) is a critical concept in assembly language programming. It defines the set of instructions that a computer's CPU can execute and the format of these instructions. Understanding the ISA of a specific CPU architecture is essential for writing assembly code that can run on that architecture. In this section, we'll explore the key aspects of ISA.

Types of Instructions

Instructions in an ISA can be categorized into several types:

1. **Data Movement Instructions:** These instructions transfer data between registers and memory or between different registers. Examples include MOV (move), PUSH (push onto the stack), and POP (pop from the stack).

2. **Arithmetic and Logical Instructions:** These instructions perform arithmetic operations (e.g., addition, subtraction) and logical operations (e.g., AND, OR) on data in registers or memory. They are fundamental for calculations and data manipulation.

3. **Control Transfer Instructions:** These instructions control the flow of execution by enabling conditional or unconditional jumps. JMP (jump) and CALL (call a subroutine) are common control transfer instructions.

4. **String Instructions:** Some architectures provide instructions for working with strings of data, such as searching, comparing, and copying. For instance, REP MOVS is used to copy a block of memory.

5. **I/O Instructions:** These instructions facilitate communication between the CPU and peripheral devices, such as reading from or writing to I/O ports.

6. **Special Instructions:** Special-purpose instructions perform specific tasks, such as enabling or disabling interrupts, changing privilege levels, or accessing coprocessors.

Instruction Formats

Each instruction in an ISA has a specific format that determines how the instruction is encoded. Common components of an instruction format include:

- **Operation Code (Opcode):** Identifies the operation to be performed, such as addition or subtraction.

- **Source Operand(s):** Specifies the source data or registers involved in the operation.

- **Destination Operand(s):** Indicates where the result of the operation should be stored.

- **Immediate Values:** Some instructions allow immediate values (constants) to be included in the instruction itself.

- **Addressing Modes:** Define how memory addresses are calculated, which can include direct addressing, indirect addressing, or indexed addressing.

The exact format and encoding of instructions vary between CPU architectures, so it's essential to refer to the architecture's documentation for precise details.

Assembly Language Mnemonics

Assembly languages use mnemonics to represent instructions in a human-readable format. Each mnemonic corresponds to a specific opcode and operation. For example, the ADD mnemonic might represent an instruction that adds two values. The assembly programmer uses mnemonics to write code, which is then assembled into machine code for execution by the CPU.

Here's an example of an assembly instruction using mnemonics:

```
ADD EAX, EBX  ; Add the values in registers EAX and EBX
```

In this instruction, ADD is the mnemonic, EAX and EBX are the operands, and the instruction represents the addition operation.

Different CPU architectures have unique ISAs with distinct features, such as the number of registers, addressing modes, and available instructions. When writing assembly code, you must adhere to the ISA of the target architecture. For example, x86 and ARM architectures have different ISAs, and code written for one cannot run directly on the other without modification.

Conclusion

The Instruction Set Architecture (ISA) is the foundation of assembly language programming. It defines the instructions available to the programmer, their formats, and how they operate on data. Understanding the ISA of your target CPU architecture is essential for writing efficient and functional assembly code. In the following sections, we will explore assembly language syntax and guide you in writing your first assembly program.

Section 2.4: Assembly Language Syntax

Assembly language has its own syntax rules and conventions that dictate how instructions and data are represented in code. Understanding assembly language syntax is crucial for writing correct and functional assembly programs. In this section, we'll explore the key aspects of assembly language syntax.

Instruction Format

In assembly language, each instruction typically follows a specific format:

```
LABEL:  OPCODE  OPERAND1, OPERAND2 ; Comment
```

- **LABEL:** An optional label that represents a memory address or a reference point in the code. Labels are used for branching and subroutine calls.

- **OPCODE:** The operation code (mnemonic) that specifies the action to be performed. Examples include MOV (move), ADD (addition), and JMP (jump).

- **OPERAND1, OPERAND2:** Zero or more operands that provide data or specify registers involved in the operation. The number and types of operands depend on the instruction.

- **Comment:** An optional comment that provides additional information about the instruction. Comments start with a semicolon (;) and are ignored by the assembler.

Here's an example of an assembly instruction:

```
LOOP_START:  MOV  AX, 1      ; Load 1 into AX
```

In this example, LOOP_START is a label, MOV is the mnemonic (opcode), AX and 1 are operands, and the comment clarifies the instruction's purpose.

Registers are typically represented by their names, which vary depending on the CPU architecture. For example, in x86 assembly, you have registers like EAX, EBX, ECX, and EDX. To reference a register, you simply use its name in the instruction. For instance:

```
MOV  EAX, EBX    ; Copy the value in EBX to EAX
```

Memory addresses are often used to specify memory locations where data is stored or retrieved. To reference a memory address, square brackets are used. For example:

```
MOV  AX, [MemoryAddress]    ; Load data from MemoryAddress into AX
```

Here, [MemoryAddress] indicates that the value should be retrieved from the memory address specified.

Directives are special instructions used by the assembler to provide additional information about the code. They are not executed by the CPU but guide the assembly process. Common directives include:

- **DB:** Define Byte - Specifies a byte of data.
- **DW:** Define Word - Specifies a 16-bit data item.
- **DD:** Define Doubleword - Specifies a 32-bit data item.
- **DQ:** Define Quadword - Specifies a 64-bit data item.
- **RESB, RESW, RESD:** Reserve Byte, Word, or Doubleword - Allocates memory space without initializing it.
- **SEGMENT:** Defines a code or data segment.

Comments in assembly language are essential for documenting your code and explaining its logic. Comments are ignored by the assembler and do not affect program execution. They are denoted by a semicolon (;) and can be placed at the end of a line or on a separate line.

```
; This is a comment
MOV  AX, 10    ; Load 10 into AX
```

Comments should be used to clarify the purpose of instructions, describe algorithms, and make the code more understandable for yourself and others.

Case Sensitivity

Assembly languages are typically case-insensitive, meaning that uppercase and lowercase letters are treated the same. However, it's a common convention to use uppercase for mnemonics and registers and lowercase for labels and variables to improve code readability.

Conclusion

Assembly language syntax forms the foundation of writing assembly code. By following the conventions and rules outlined in this section, you can create clear and functional assembly programs. As you progress in assembly programming, you'll become more familiar with the specific syntax of the architecture you're working with and be able to write more complex and efficient code. In the following sections, we will guide you in writing your first assembly program and provide practical examples to reinforce your understanding of assembly language.

Section 2.5: Writing Your First Assembly Program

Now that you have a basic understanding of assembly language syntax and the key components of instructions, it's time to write your first assembly program. This introductory program will help you become familiar with the process of writing, assembling, and running assembly code.

Development Environment Setup

Before you start writing assembly code, ensure that you have a development environment set up with the necessary tools. This includes a text editor or integrated development environment (IDE) for writing code, an assembler for converting your assembly code into machine code, and a debugger for testing and troubleshooting.

Hello, World! in Assembly

Let's begin with a classic "Hello, World!" program in assembly language. This program will print the "Hello, World!" message to the console. The exact code will depend on the architecture you're working with, but we'll use x86 assembly for this example.

Here's a simple x86 assembly program to print "Hello, World!" using the DOS interrupt:

```
section .data
    hello db 'Hello, World!',0  ; Null-terminated string

section .text
    global _start

_start:
    ; Write "Hello, World!" to stdout (file descriptor 1)
    mov eax, 4
```

```
mov ebx, 1
mov ecx, hello
mov edx, 13
int 0x80

; Exit the program
mov eax, 1
int 0x80
```

This program consists of two sections: .data and .text. The .data section defines the null-terminated string "Hello, World!" that we want to print. The .text section contains the actual code.

In the .text section, we use x86 assembly instructions to write the message to the standard output (stdout) and then exit the program.

Assembling and Running the Program

To assemble and run the program, follow these steps:

1. Save the assembly code in a file with a .asm extension, such as hello.asm.

2. Open a terminal or command prompt and navigate to the directory containing your assembly code.

3. Assemble the code using an assembler specific to your architecture. For x86 on Linux, you can use the nasm assembler:

    ```
    nasm -f elf hello.asm -o hello.o
    ```

4. Link the object file to create an executable:

    ```
    ld hello.o -o hello
    ```

5. Run the program:

    ```
    ./hello
    ```

You should see "Hello, World!" printed to the console.

Understanding the Code

Let's briefly explain the key parts of the assembly code:

*   The .data section defines the string "Hello, World!" as a null-terminated string (hello db 'Hello, World!',0).

*   The .text section contains the program's code. It starts with the _start label, which is the program's entry point.

*   We use the mov instruction to set up registers with the necessary values. For example, mov eax, 4 sets eax to 4, which is the code for the write system call.

- The `int 0x80` instruction triggers a software interrupt to invoke the operating system's functionality. In this case, it's used to write the message to the console.

- After printing the message, the program exits by calling the `exit` system call (`mov eax, 1` and `int 0x80`).

Experiment and Explore

Congratulations! You've written and run your first assembly program. To deepen your understanding, consider making modifications to the code. Try printing a different message, adding comments, or experimenting with other x86 assembly instructions. As you gain more experience, you'll be able to tackle more complex assembly programming tasks and projects.

Chapter 3: Flow Control and Branching

Section 3.1: Conditional Branching

Conditional branching is a fundamental concept in assembly language programming that allows you to control the flow of execution based on specific conditions. In this section, we'll explore conditional branching instructions and how they are used in assembly programming.

Conditional Branching Instructions

Conditional branching instructions enable your program to make decisions and execute different code paths based on the evaluation of a condition. These instructions are often used in conjunction with comparison and test operations to determine whether a particular condition is true or false.

Common conditional branching instructions include:

- **JZ (Jump if Zero) / JE (Jump if Equal):** These instructions jump to a specified label if the Zero (ZF) flag is set, indicating that the result of a previous operation was zero or that two values are equal.

- **JNZ (Jump if Not Zero) / JNE (Jump if Not Equal):** These instructions jump if the Zero (ZF) flag is not set, indicating that the result was not zero or that two values are not equal.

- **JG (Jump if Greater):** Jumps if the Zero (ZF) flag is not set and the Sign (SF) and Overflow (OF) flags are the same, indicating that the value in the source operand is greater.

- **JGE (Jump if Greater or Equal):** Jumps if the Zero (ZF) flag is not set, or if the Sign (SF) and Overflow (OF) flags are the same or the Zero (ZF) flag is set, indicating that the value in the source operand is greater or equal.

- **JL (Jump if Less):** Jumps if the Zero (ZF) flag is not set and the Sign (SF) and Overflow (OF) flags are different, indicating that the value in the source operand is less.

- **JLE (Jump if Less or Equal):** Jumps if the Zero (ZF) flag is set, or if the Sign (SF) and Overflow (OF) flags are different, indicating that the value in the source operand is less or equal.

Example: Conditional Branching in Assembly

Let's illustrate conditional branching with a simple x86 assembly example. In this program, we'll compare two values and print a message based on the comparison result.

```
section .data
    message1 db 'Value1 is greater', 0
    message2 db 'Value2 is greater', 0

section .text
    global _start

_start:
    ; Assume Value1 and Value2 are loaded into registers EAX and EBX

    ; Compare EAX (Value1) and EBX (Value2)
    cmp eax, ebx

    ; Check if EAX > EBX (ZF=0 and SF=OF)
    jg greater

    ; If not greater, EAX <= EBX
    ; Print "Value2 is greater" and exit
    mov eax, 4
    mov ebx, 1
    mov ecx, message2
    mov edx, 17
    int 0x80
    jmp done

greater:
    ; Print "Value1 is greater" and exit
    mov eax, 4
    mov ebx, 1
    mov ecx, message1
    mov edx, 17
    int 0x80

done:
    ; Exit the program
    mov eax, 1
    int 0x80
```

In this example, we compare the values in registers EAX and EBX using the cmp instruction. Depending on the comparison result, we use the jg instruction to jump to the greater label or continue to the code that prints the message for the case when the second value is greater. Finally, we exit the program.

Section 3.2: Unconditional Jump Instructions

Unconditional jump instructions are a vital part of assembly language programming, allowing you to control the flow of execution by directing the program to jump to a specific location in the code. Unlike conditional branches, unconditional jumps do not depend on conditions or flags; they simply transfer control to the target address. In this section, we'll explore unconditional jump instructions and their uses in assembly programming.

Unconditional jump instructions provide a way to change the program's execution flow without regard to any condition. Common unconditional jump instructions include:

- **JMP (Jump):** This instruction unconditionally transfers control to a specified label or memory address.

- **CALL (Call Subroutine):** Similar to JMP, but it also pushes the return address onto the stack, allowing the program to return to the calling point later.

- **RET (Return):** Used to return from a subroutine. It pops the return address from the stack and transfers control to that address.

- **JMP to Register/Pointer:** Some architectures support jumping to an address stored in a register or memory location.

Use Cases for Unconditional Jumps

Unconditional jumps are used for various purposes in assembly programming:

1. **Implementing Loops:** Unconditional jumps are often used to create loops in assembly programs. You can use a combination of labels and jumps to repeat a block of code until a specific condition is met.

2. **Function Calls and Subroutines:** When calling a subroutine or function, you typically use a CALL instruction to transfer control to the subroutine. The RET instruction is used within the subroutine to return control to the calling point.

3. **Handling Exceptions:** In some cases, when an exceptional condition occurs, an unconditional jump might be used to transfer control to an exception handling routine.

4. **Jump Tables:** Unconditional jumps can be used to implement jump tables, which are arrays of addresses that point to different sections of code. Depending on input or conditions, you can jump to a specific section of code.

Example: Implementing a Loop

Let's illustrate the use of an unconditional jump to implement a simple loop in x86 assembly. In this example, we'll write a program to print numbers from 1 to 10.

```
section .text
    global _start

_start:
    mov ecx, 1          ; Initialize counter (ECX) to 1
```

```
print_loop:
    ; Print the value in ECX
    mov eax, 4
    mov ebx, 1
    mov edx, 1
    mov esi, ecx
    add esi, '0'      ; Convert the counter value to ASCII
    mov ecx, esi
    int 0x80

    ; Increment counter
    inc ecx

    ; Check if counter reached 11 (end of loop)
    cmp ecx, 11
    jnz print_loop    ; If not equal, jump back to print_loop

exit_program:
    ; Exit the program
    mov eax, 1
    int 0x80
```

In this code, we initialize a counter (ECX) to 1 and enter a loop labeled print_loop. Inside the loop, we print the value of the counter, increment it, and then check if it has reached 11. If not, we use the jnz (Jump if Not Zero) instruction to jump back to the print_loop label, effectively creating a loop that prints numbers from 1 to 10. When the counter reaches 11, we exit the program.

Unconditional jumps are powerful tools in assembly programming that allow you to create flexible and structured code by controlling the program's flow. They are essential for implementing loops, function calls, and managing program execution in various scenarios.

Section 3.3: Looping and Iteration

Looping and iteration are fundamental concepts in assembly language programming, allowing you to repeat a block of code multiple times. In this section, we'll explore various looping techniques and instructions commonly used in assembly programming.

Using Conditional Branching for Loops

Conditional branching instructions, such as JZ (Jump if Zero) and JNZ (Jump if Not Zero), are often used to implement loops in assembly. Here's a simple example of a loop that prints numbers from 1 to 10 using x86 assembly:

```
section .text
    global _start
```

```
_start:
    mov ecx, 1          ; Initialize counter (ECX) to 1

print_loop:
    ; Print the value in ECX
    mov eax, 4
    mov ebx, 1
    mov edx, 1
    mov esi, ecx
    add esi, '0'        ; Convert the counter value to ASCII
    mov ecx, esi
    int 0x80

    ; Increment counter
    inc ecx

    ; Check if counter reached 11 (end of loop)
    cmp ecx, 11
    jnz print_loop      ; If not equal, jump back to print_loop

exit_program:
    ; Exit the program
    mov eax, 1
    int 0x80
```

In this example, we use the cmp instruction to compare the value in the ECX register (counter) with 11, and if they are not equal (jnz), we jump back to the print_loop label to repeat the printing and incrementing steps. This creates a loop that prints numbers from 1 to 10.

Using Unconditional Jumps for Loops

Unconditional jumps, such as JMP (Jump) and LOOP, can also be used to create loops in assembly. Here's an example of a loop that counts down from 10 to 1 using the LOOP instruction in x86 assembly:

```
section .text
    global _start

_start:
    mov ecx, 10         ; Initialize counter (ECX) to 10

print_loop:
    ; Print the value in ECX
    mov eax, 4
    mov ebx, 1
    mov edx, 1
    mov esi, ecx
```

```
    add esi, '0'      ; Convert the counter value to ASCII
    mov ecx, esi
    int 0x80

    ; Decrement counter and check if it's greater than 0
    loop print_loop   ; Decrement ECX and jump if ECX > 0

exit_program:
    ; Exit the program
    mov eax, 1
    int 0x80
```

In this example, we use the LOOP instruction, which automatically decrements the ECX register and jumps back to the print_loop label as long as ECX is greater than 0. This creates a loop that counts down from 10 to 1.

Conditional vs. Unconditional Loops

Both conditional and unconditional loops have their uses in assembly programming. Conditional loops are suitable when you need to repeat a block of code a specific number of times or based on a condition. Unconditional loops, like the LOOP instruction, are convenient when you want to repeat a block of code a fixed number of times.

Conclusion

Loops and iteration are essential for performing repetitive tasks in assembly language programming. Whether you choose conditional or unconditional loops depends on your specific requirements and the structure of your program. Understanding loop constructs and how to use them effectively is a key skill for assembly programmers.

Section 3.4: Subroutines and Function Calls

Subroutines and function calls are essential in assembly language programming for organizing and reusing code. In this section, we'll explore how to define and call subroutines, including parameter passing and return values.

Subroutine Basics

A subroutine, also known as a function or procedure, is a self-contained block of code that performs a specific task. Subroutines are used to modularize code, making it more readable, maintainable, and reusable. In assembly, a subroutine is defined by a sequence of instructions enclosed within labels.

Here's a simple example of a subroutine in x86 assembly that calculates the square of a number:

```
section .text
    global _start
```

```
_start:
    mov eax, 5        ; Load a value (5) into EAX
    call square       ; Call the square subroutine

    ; The result is now in EAX
    ; You can use it as needed

exit_program:
    ; Exit the program
    mov eax, 1
    int 0x80

square:
    ; Input: EAX (the number to square)
    ; Output: EAX (the squared result)

    imul eax, eax     ; Multiply EAX by itself to calculate the square
    ret               ; Return from the subroutine
```

In this example, we define a square subroutine that takes a single input parameter in the EAX register, calculates the square of the number, and returns the result in EAX. The _start section of the program calls the square subroutine by using the call instruction, passing the value 5 in EAX. After the subroutine finishes, the squared result is available in EAX.

Parameter Passing and Return Values

In assembly, parameters are typically passed to subroutines through registers or the stack. In the example above, we passed the input parameter in the EAX register. The subroutine modified the value in EAX to return the result.

Return values are commonly placed in registers designated for this purpose, such as EAX. The ret instruction is used to return from a subroutine, and it automatically pops the return address from the stack.

Stacks and the CALL/RET Mechanism

Subroutines often rely on the stack to manage data and return addresses. When a subroutine is called using call, the current program counter (the address of the instruction following the call instruction) is pushed onto the stack as the return address. The ret instruction later pops this return address from the stack and transfers control back to the calling point.

Here's a basic illustration of the stack during a subroutine call:

```
Stack before call:
...
Return Address   <--- Top of the stack
...
```

```
Instructions:
...
call subroutine
...

Stack after call:
...
Return Address   <--- Top of the stack
Old EBP
...
```

Using the Stack for Local Variables

The stack is also used for managing local variables within subroutines. By adjusting the stack pointer (ESP on x86), you can allocate space for local variables and deallocate it when the subroutine exits. This stack-based approach allows for dynamic memory allocation within subroutines.

Conclusion

Subroutines and function calls are crucial for organizing and reusing code in assembly programming. They allow you to create modular and maintainable code by encapsulating specific functionality. Understanding parameter passing, return values, and the stack-based CALL/RET mechanism is essential for effectively working with subroutines in assembly.

Section 3.5: Error Handling and Exception Handling

Error handling and exception handling are critical aspects of assembly language programming, as they allow programs to respond to unexpected events and errors gracefully. In this section, we'll explore how to handle errors and exceptions in assembly programming.

Error Handling Techniques

Error handling in assembly typically involves identifying and responding to exceptional conditions that may arise during program execution. Common error handling techniques include:

1. **Conditional Branching:** Using conditional branch instructions (JZ, JNZ, etc.) to check for specific error conditions and take appropriate actions based on those conditions.

2. **Error Codes:** Storing error codes in specific registers or memory locations to indicate the nature of the error. Error codes can be checked and acted upon as needed.

3. **Interrupts:** Leveraging software interrupts to trigger error-handling routines or to communicate with the operating system for error reporting.

4. **Exception Handling:** Handling exceptions that arise from issues like division by zero, invalid memory access, or other exceptional events using exception handling mechanisms provided by the CPU architecture or the operating system.

Exception Handling

Exception handling in assembly is a mechanism for gracefully handling exceptional conditions or errors that occur during program execution. Exceptions can be triggered by various events, such as divide-by-zero, invalid memory access, or hardware interrupts. The assembly language provides instructions and mechanisms for dealing with exceptions.

Here's an example of handling a divide-by-zero exception in x86 assembly:

```
section .text
    global _start

_start:
    mov eax, 10        ; Numerator
    mov ebx, 0         ; Denominator

    ; Check if the denominator is zero
    cmp ebx, 0
    jz divide_error    ; Jump to divide_error if zero

    ; Perform the division
    div ebx

    ; Handle the result or continue with normal execution
    ; ...

exit_program:
    ; Exit the program
    mov eax, 1
    int 0x80

divide_error:
    ; Handle the divide-by-zero error
    ; Display an error message, log the error, or take appropriate action
    ; Then exit the program
    ; ...
```

In this example, we attempt to divide a number by zero. Before performing the division, we check if the denominator (ebx) is zero using conditional branching (jz). If it's zero, we jump to the divide_error label to handle the divide-by-zero error.

Using Interrupts for Exception Handling

Many exceptional conditions in assembly programming can be handled using software interrupts (int instruction). The operating system typically provides interrupt service routines (ISRs) that can handle various exceptions. When an exceptional condition occurs, you can trigger the appropriate interrupt to invoke the corresponding ISR.

For example, in x86 assembly, you can trigger a divide-by-zero exception by using the `int 0` instruction. The CPU will then call the corresponding ISR defined by the operating system to handle the exception.

Custom Exception Handling

In some cases, you may need to implement custom exception handling routines in assembly. This can involve setting up exception vectors, defining custom ISRs, and specifying how to respond to specific exceptions. Custom exception handling is often required in system programming and low-level development.

Conclusion

Error handling and exception handling are essential aspects of assembly programming for ensuring the robustness and reliability of software. Depending on the nature of the program and the exceptional conditions it may encounter, you can use conditional branching, error codes, software interrupts, or custom exception handling to gracefully respond to errors and exceptions. Understanding how to handle errors and exceptions is vital for writing robust and reliable assembly programs.

Chapter 4: Data Manipulation

Section 4.1: Data Movement Instructions

Data movement instructions in assembly language are fundamental for copying and transferring data between registers, memory locations, and other data storage areas. In this section, we will explore data movement instructions and their significance in assembly programming.

Data Movement Operations

Data movement instructions allow you to perform various operations, including:

1. **Load:** Loading data from memory or a specific location into a register. This is often used to access variables or constants.

2. **Store:** Storing data from a register into memory. This is essential for updating variables or saving results.

3. **Transfer:** Copying data from one register to another. This is useful for rearranging data or making multiple copies.

4. **Immediate Load:** Loading an immediate value (a constant) directly into a register. This is often used for setting up initial values or performing calculations.

Example: Moving Data in x86 Assembly

In x86 assembly, data movement instructions are commonly used. Here's an example that demonstrates some data movement instructions:

```
section .data
    message db 'Hello, Assembly!',0  ; Null-terminated string
    num1 dd 42                        ; Doubleword (4 bytes) variable

section .text
    global _start

_start:
    ; Load data from memory into registers
    mov eax, num1      ; Load the value of num1 into EAX

    ; Store data from a register into memory
    mov ebx, 99        ; Load the value 99 into EBX
    mov [num1], ebx    ; Store the value in EBX into num1

    ; Transfer data between registers
    mov ecx, eax       ; Copy the value of EAX into ECX
```

```
  ; Immediate load
  mov edx, 123        ; Load the immediate value 123 into EDX

  ; ...

exit_program:
  ; Exit the program
  mov eax, 1
  int 0x80
```

In this example, we load data from the num1 variable into the EAX register using the mov instruction. We also store the value 99 from the EBX register back into the num1 variable. Data is transferred from EAX to ECX using another mov instruction, and we load the immediate value 123 into the EDX register.

These operations allow you to manipulate data efficiently, which is essential for performing calculations, working with variables, and controlling program flow.

Data Sizes and Types

It's important to note that data movement instructions are size-specific. For example, x86 assembly provides different instructions for moving byte-sized, word-sized, doubleword-sized, or quadword-sized data. Properly selecting the instruction that matches the data size is crucial for correct and efficient data manipulation.

Addressing Modes

Data movement instructions can also be combined with various addressing modes to access data stored in memory efficiently. Common addressing modes include direct addressing, indirect addressing, and indexed addressing.

Conclusion

Data movement instructions are the building blocks of assembly programming, allowing you to manipulate and transfer data efficiently. Understanding how to load, store, transfer, and use data is essential for writing effective assembly programs. These instructions are fundamental for working with variables, constants, and other data elements in your code.

Section 4.2: Arithmetic and Logical Operations

Arithmetic and logical operations are fundamental in assembly language programming for performing mathematical calculations and logical evaluations. In this section, we'll delve into arithmetic and logical instructions and how they are employed in assembly programming.

Arithmetic Operations

Arithmetic instructions allow you to perform various mathematical operations on data stored in registers or memory locations. Common arithmetic operations include addition, subtraction, multiplication, division, and more. Here are a few examples of arithmetic operations in x86 assembly:

Addition:
```
add eax, ebx  ; Add the value in EBX to EAX
```

Subtraction:
```
sub ecx, edx  ; Subtract the value in EDX from ECX
```

Multiplication:
```
imul esi, edi, 3  ; Multiply the value in EDI by 3 and store the result in ES
I
```

Division:
```
idiv eax, ecx  ; Divide the value in EAX by ECX, result in EAX, remainder in
EDX
```

Logical Operations

Logical instructions are used to manipulate individual bits within registers or memory locations. Common logical operations include bitwise AND, OR, XOR (exclusive OR), and NOT. These operations are often used for data masking, setting or clearing specific bits, and other bit-level operations. Here are some examples:

Bitwise AND:
```
and eax, ebx  ; Perform a bitwise AND operation between EAX and EBX
```

Bitwise OR:
```
or ecx, edx  ; Perform a bitwise OR operation between ECX and EDX
```

Bitwise XOR:
```
xor esi, edi  ; Perform a bitwise XOR operation between ESI and EDI
```

Bitwise NOT:
```
not eax        ; Perform a bitwise NOT operation on EAX
```

Conditional Instructions

Arithmetic and logical instructions are often used in combination with conditional branching instructions to make decisions and control program flow based on the results of these operations. For example, you can use a comparison followed by a conditional jump to execute specific code only when a certain condition is met.

```
cmp eax, ebx       ; Compare EAX and EBX
je equal_label     ; Jump to equal_label if they are equal
jne not_equal_label; Jump to not_equal_label if they are not equal
```

Overflow and Flags

Arithmetic operations may set flags in the processor's status register to indicate conditions such as overflow, carry, zero, and sign. These flags can be checked using conditional instructions to respond to specific conditions during program execution.

Conclusion

Arithmetic and logical operations are crucial for performing calculations and making logical evaluations in assembly programming. These operations, when combined with conditional branching, allow you to create flexible and powerful algorithms. Understanding how to use arithmetic and logical instructions and interpret flags is essential for writing effective assembly programs that perform mathematical computations and logical decisions.

Section 4.3: Bit Manipulation

Bit manipulation is a fundamental concept in assembly language programming that involves working with individual bits within data. In this section, we'll explore the importance of bit manipulation and the instructions used for this purpose.

Bitwise Logical Operations

Bitwise logical operations, including AND, OR, XOR, and NOT, are fundamental for bit manipulation in assembly. These operations enable you to manipulate specific bits within data, set or clear individual bits, and perform various masking and filtering operations.

For example, if you want to set the 5th bit (counting from the least significant bit) of a register to 1 while keeping the other bits unchanged, you can use the bitwise OR operation:

```
or eax, 0x20   ; Set the 5th bit (0x20 in hexadecimal) to 1
```

Conversely, you can clear the same bit by using the bitwise AND operation with a mask:

```
and eax, 0xFFFFFFDF   ; Clear the 5th bit by masking with 0xFFFFFFDF
```

Shifting and Rotating Bits

Shifting and rotating instructions are crucial for moving bits within a data value. These instructions allow you to shift bits left or right or perform circular rotations.

- **Shift Left (SHL/SHR):** The shift left (SHL) and shift right (SHR) instructions move bits in the specified direction, filling the vacant bits with zeros.

```
shl eax, 1   ; Shift all bits in EAX one position to the left
shr ebx, 3   ; Shift all bits in EBX three positions to the right
```

- **Rotate Left (ROL/ROR):** The rotate left (ROL) and rotate right (ROR) instructions move bits circularly, with bits shifted out on one side reappearing on the opposite side.

```
rol ecx, 4    ; Rotate all bits in ECX four positions to the left
ror edx, 2    ; Rotate all bits in EDX two positions to the right
```

Bit Testing and Setting

Bit testing instructions allow you to check the value of a specific bit without modifying the data. For instance, you can use the test instruction to check if a particular bit is set:

```
test esi, 0x08    ; Test if the 4th bit (0x08 in hexadecimal) of ESI is set
```

You can also use bit manipulation to set or clear specific bits based on conditions. For example, you can set a bit if a certain condition is met using a combination of bitwise OR and conditional branching.

Bit Manipulation for Flags

Bit manipulation is often used to interact with and manipulate processor flags, such as the zero flag (ZF) or carry flag (CF). These flags are essential for making decisions and controlling program flow based on the results of arithmetic and logical operations.

Conclusion

Bit manipulation is a fundamental skill in assembly programming, allowing you to work with individual bits within data effectively. Whether you need to set, clear, shift, rotate, or test bits, understanding how to perform bit manipulation operations is essential for solving various programming challenges and optimizing your assembly code.

Section 4.4: String Manipulation

String manipulation is a fundamental aspect of assembly language programming, especially when dealing with text-based data. In this section, we'll explore how assembly languages handle strings, including techniques for copying, searching, and manipulating character strings.

String Representation

In assembly, strings are typically represented as sequences of characters stored in memory. Each character is usually encoded using the ASCII or UTF-8 character encoding, where each character corresponds to a numerical value.

For example, the string "Hello, Assembly!" would be stored in memory as a sequence of bytes, each byte representing the ASCII code for the corresponding character:

```
48 65 6C 6C 6F 2C 20 41 73 73 65 6D 62 6C 79 21
```

String Copying

Copying a string from one memory location to another is a common operation in assembly programming. This can be accomplished using string copy instructions or by iterating through each character and copying them individually.

For example, in x86 assembly, you can use the rep movsb instruction to copy a block of memory from one location to another efficiently:

```
section .data
    source db 'Hello, Assembly!',0
    dest   db 20 dup(0)  ; Allocate space for the destination string

section .text
    global _start

_start:
    mov esi, source    ; Source address
    mov edi, dest      ; Destination address
    cld                ; Clear direction flag (forward direction)
    mov ecx, 20        ; Number of bytes to copy (including the null terminato
r)
    rep movsb          ; Copy ECX bytes from DS:[ESI] to ES:[EDI]

    ; The 'dest' buffer now contains a copy of the 'source' string

exit_program:
    ; Exit the program
    mov eax, 1
    int 0x80
```

In this example, the rep movsb instruction is used to copy the entire string from the source to the destination. The cld instruction ensures that the direction flag is cleared to perform the copy in the forward direction.

String Manipulation and Searching

Manipulating strings in assembly often involves searching for specific characters or substrings, replacing characters, or performing other text-processing tasks. These operations are typically implemented using loops and conditional branching.

For example, here's a simple x86 assembly program that counts the number of occurrences of a specific character ('e') in a string:

```
section .data
    str db 'Hello, Assembly!',0
    search_char db 'e'

section .text
    global _start
```

```
_start:
    mov esi, str          ; Source string address
    mov al, [search_char]  ; Character to search for
    xor ecx, ecx          ; Initialize counter to zero

search_loop:
    lodsb                  ; Load the next character from [ESI] into AL
    cmp al, 0              ; Check if it's the null terminator (end of string)
    je exit_program        ; If yes, exit the loop
    cmp al, [search_char]  ; Compare AL with the character to search for
    jne continue_search ; If not equal, continue searching
    inc ecx                ; Increment the counter for a match

continue_search:
    jmp search_loop       ; Continue searching

exit_program:
    ; The 'ecx' register now contains the count of 'e' characters in the string

    ; Exit the program
    mov eax, 1
    int 0x80
```

In this program, we use a loop to iterate through the characters in the string and compare each character with the target character ('e'). If a match is found, we increment a counter (ecx). The loop continues until the null terminator is encountered, indicating the end of the string.

String Manipulation for Text Processing

String manipulation techniques can be used for a wide range of text-processing tasks, such as tokenization, parsing, and formatting. By understanding how to work with strings in assembly, you gain the ability to process and manipulate text data efficiently, which is essential in various application domains.

Conclusion

String manipulation is a crucial skill in assembly programming, enabling you to work with text-based data effectively. Whether you need to copy, search, or manipulate strings, understanding the principles and techniques for string handling is essential for creating assembly programs that work with textual information.

Section 4.5: Working with Data Structures

Working with data structures is a fundamental aspect of assembly language programming, allowing you to organize and manage complex data efficiently. In this section, we'll explore how assembly languages handle data structures and the techniques involved.

Data Structures in Assembly

Data structures are collections of data elements organized in a specific way for efficient access and modification. Common data structures include arrays, linked lists, stacks, queues, and trees. In assembly, these data structures are typically implemented using arrays, pointers, and custom memory layouts.

Arrays

Arrays are one of the simplest forms of data structures and can be easily implemented in assembly. They consist of a contiguous block of memory locations, each holding an element of the same data type. Accessing elements in an array involves simple address calculations.

Here's an example of defining and accessing an array in x86 assembly:

```
section .data
    my_array dd 10, 20, 30, 40, 50  ; An array of doublewords

section .text
    global _start

_start:
    ; Accessing elements in the array
    mov eax, [my_array]      ; Load the first element (10) into EAX
    mov ebx, [my_array+4]    ; Load the second element (20) into EBX
    ; ...

exit_program:
    ; Exit the program
    mov eax, 1
    int 0x80
```

Pointers

Pointers are essential in assembly for managing dynamic data structures like linked lists, trees, and dynamically allocated memory. Pointers hold memory addresses, allowing you to access data indirectly. For example, you can use pointers to traverse a linked list or dynamically allocate memory for new data.

Here's a simple example of using a pointer in x86 assembly to access data indirectly:

```
section .data
    my_var dd 42       ; A doubleword variable
    my_ptr dd 0        ; A pointer variable

section .text
    global _start

_start:
    ; Initializing the pointer
    mov esi, my_var    ; Load the address of 'my_var' into ESI
    mov [my_ptr], esi ; Store the address in 'my_ptr'

    ; Accessing data indirectly through the pointer
    mov eax, [esi]     ; Load the value at the address in ESI (42) into EAX
    mov ebx, [my_ptr] ; Load the address from 'my_ptr' into EBX
    mov ecx, [ebx]     ; Load the value at the address in EBX (42) into ECX

    ; ...

exit_program:
    ; Exit the program
    mov eax, 1
    int 0x80
```

Custom Data Structures

Assembly languages provide the flexibility to define custom data structures using arrays, structures, or other combinations of data elements. For instance, you can define a structure that represents a complex data type and access its members individually.

```
section .data
    my_struct:
        field1 dd 10
        field2 dd 20

section .text
    global _start

_start:
    ; Accessing structure members
    mov eax, [my_struct.field1] ; Load the value 10 into EAX
    mov ebx, [my_struct.field2] ; Load the value 20 into EBX

    ; ...

exit_program:
    ; Exit the program
    mov eax, 1
    int 0x80
```

Conclusion

Working with data structures is essential in assembly programming to manage and organize data efficiently. Whether you're dealing with arrays, pointers, or custom data layouts, understanding how to manipulate and access data structures is crucial for writing effective assembly programs that handle complex data and perform advanced operations.

Chapter 5: Memory Management

Section 5.1: Memory Addressing Modes

Memory addressing modes are essential in assembly language programming for specifying the location of data operands in memory. These addressing modes determine how the effective address of an operand is calculated, allowing you to access data efficiently and flexibly.

Direct Addressing

Direct addressing is the simplest addressing mode, where the operand's memory location is explicitly specified. The effective address is the memory address provided in the instruction. For example:

```
mov eax, [0x12345678]   ; Load the value from memory address 0x12345678 into E
AX
```

In this example, the effective address is 0x12345678, and the data at that address is loaded into the EAX register.

Register Indirect Addressing

Register indirect addressing involves specifying a register that contains the memory address of the operand. The effective address is obtained from the content of the specified register. For instance:

```
mov ecx, [ebx]   ; Load the value from the memory address stored in EBX into E
CX
```

In this case, the EBX register holds the memory address, and the data at that address is loaded into the ECX register.

Immediate Addressing

Immediate addressing mode involves specifying a constant value as an operand directly within the instruction. There is no memory access in this mode. For example:

```
mov edx, 42   ; Load the immediate value 42 into the EDX register
```

The operand, in this case, is the constant 42, and it is directly loaded into the EDX register without memory access.

Displacement Addressing

Displacement addressing combines an immediate value (displacement) with a base register to calculate the effective address. It is useful for accessing data in data structures like arrays and structures. Here's an example:

```
mov esi, [ebx + 8]   ; Load the value at the memory address [EBX + 8] into ESI
```

In this example, the effective address is calculated by adding 8 to the content of the EBX register.

Scaled Index Addressing

Scaled index addressing mode involves using an index register, a base register, and a scaling factor to calculate the effective address. It is often used in array traversal and data structure access. Here's an example:

```
mov edx, [ebx + esi*4]   ; Load the value at the memory address [EBX + ESI*4]
into EDX
```

In this case, the effective address is calculated by adding the content of EBX and four times the content of ESI.

Base-Indexed Displacement Addressing

This addressing mode combines a base register, an index register, and an immediate displacement to calculate the effective address. It offers flexibility in accessing data in structured memory layouts. For example:

```
mov eax, [ebx + esi*2 + 12]   ; Load the value at the memory address [EBX + ES
I*2 + 12] into EAX
```

Here, the effective address is determined by the sum of the content of EBX, two times the content of ESI, and the constant 12.

Conclusion

Memory addressing modes in assembly language provide a powerful way to specify the location of data operands in memory. These modes enable efficient and flexible memory access, making it possible to work with various data structures and perform complex memory operations in assembly programs. Understanding and utilizing different addressing modes is essential for effective memory management in assembly programming.

Section 5.2: Stack Operations

The stack is a crucial data structure in assembly language programming and plays a significant role in managing program execution and memory. This section explores stack operations, their importance, and how they are used in assembly programming.

What is the Stack?

The stack is a region of memory used for temporary storage and management of data during program execution. It operates on the Last-In, First-Out (LIFO) principle, meaning that the last item pushed onto the stack is the first item popped off. The stack is typically used for storing function call information, local variables, and return addresses.

In x86 assembly, the ESP (Extended Stack Pointer) or RSP (64-bit) register points to the top of the stack, while the EBP (Extended Base Pointer) or RBP (64-bit) register is often used as a frame pointer to access local variables and function parameters within a function's stack frame.

Here's an example of setting up a simple stack frame in x86 assembly:

```
push ebp          ; Save the previous base pointer
mov ebp, esp      ; Set the current stack pointer as the new base pointer
sub esp, 20       ; Allocate space for local variables (e.g., 20 bytes)
```

In this code, we push the previous base pointer onto the stack, set the current stack pointer as the new base pointer, and allocate space for local variables by subtracting from ESP.

Stack operations involve pushing (placing data onto the stack) and popping (removing data from the stack) values onto and from the stack. The push and pop instructions are used for these operations.

Here's an example of pushing and popping values onto and from the stack:

```
push eax          ; Push the value in EAX onto the stack
pop ebx           ; Pop the top value from the stack into EBX
```

These operations are commonly used for saving and restoring registers or passing function parameters.

Function calls and returns are essential parts of program execution, and the stack is instrumental in managing them. The call instruction pushes the return address onto the stack and transfers control to the called function, while the ret instruction pops the return address from the stack, allowing the program to return to the calling function.

```
call my_function    ; Call the function 'my_function'
...
my_function:
    ; Function code here
    ret              ; Return to the caller
```

A stack frame is a section of the stack used by a specific function during its execution. It contains local variables, function parameters, and the return address. The base pointer (EBP/RBP) is typically used to access the stack frame.

```
push ebp            ; Save the previous base pointer
mov ebp, esp        ; Set the current stack pointer as the new base pointer
sub esp, 20         ; Allocate space for local variables (e.g., 20 bytes)

; Accessing local variables and function parameters using EBP
mov eax, [ebp-4] ; Access a local variable
```

Stack Overflow and Underflow

Stack operations must be managed carefully to avoid stack overflow (exceeding available stack space) and underflow (popping from an empty stack), which can lead to program crashes and instability. Properly balancing push and pop operations and ensuring that stack space is appropriately allocated are crucial for preventing these issues.

Conclusion

Stack operations are fundamental in assembly programming for managing program execution, local variables, and function calls. Understanding how the stack works, its conventions, and its role in function calls is essential for writing efficient and correct assembly programs.

Section 5.3: Memory Allocation and Deallocation

Memory management is a critical aspect of assembly language programming, especially when it comes to allocating and deallocating memory dynamically. This section delves into the concepts and techniques of memory allocation and deallocation in assembly programming.

Static vs. Dynamic Memory

In assembly programming, memory can be categorized into two main types: static and dynamic.

- **Static Memory:** Static memory allocation refers to the allocation of memory at compile-time or program startup. Memory for global variables and statically declared arrays is allocated statically and remains constant throughout the program's execution.

- **Dynamic Memory:** Dynamic memory allocation occurs during program execution, allowing you to request memory as needed. This memory is allocated from a region known as the heap. Dynamic memory allocation is essential when you need to work with data structures of variable size or when you don't know the memory requirements beforehand.

Memory Allocation Functions

In many assembly languages, dynamic memory allocation is facilitated by system calls or library functions provided by the operating system. For example, in x86 assembly, you can use the `malloc` and `free` functions from the C Standard Library for memory allocation and deallocation.

Here's a simplified example of using `malloc` in x86 assembly to allocate memory:

```
section .data
    mem_size dd 16  ; Size of memory to allocate (e.g., 16 bytes)

section .text
    global _start

_start:
    ; Call malloc to allocate memory
    mov eax, 4      ; Function code for malloc (4)
    mov ebx, [mem_size]  ; Size of memory to allocate
    int 0x80        ; Call kernel

    ; The address of the allocated memory is now in EAX

    ; ... (use the allocated memory)

    ; Call free to deallocate memory when done
    mov eax, 1      ; Function code for free (1)
    int 0x80        ; Call kernel to release memory

    ; Exit the program
    mov eax, 1
    int 0x80
```

In this example, we use the `malloc` system call (function code 4) to allocate memory and the `free` system call (function code 1) to deallocate it. The address of the allocated memory is returned in the `EAX` register.

Memory Leak Prevention

When dynamically allocating memory, it's crucial to deallocate it properly when it's no longer needed to prevent memory leaks. Failing to free memory can lead to the gradual consumption of available memory and eventual program instability.

Stack vs. Heap

In assembly programming, both stack and heap memory play distinct roles. Stack memory is used for function call frames and has a limited size, while heap memory is more flexible but requires explicit allocation and deallocation. Choosing between stack and heap memory depends on the program's requirements and memory management strategy.

Memory Management Challenges

Dynamic memory management in assembly comes with its set of challenges, such as ensuring proper deallocation, avoiding memory fragmentation, and handling allocation failures gracefully. These challenges require careful consideration and coding practices to maintain program stability and reliability.

Conclusion

Memory allocation and deallocation are essential aspects of assembly language programming, allowing programs to manage memory dynamically and efficiently. Understanding the concepts of dynamic memory allocation, using appropriate memory management functions or system calls, and practicing proper memory management techniques are crucial for writing robust assembly programs.

Section 5.4: Memory-Mapped I/O

Memory-mapped I/O is a technique used in assembly language programming to interact with hardware devices by treating them as if they were memory locations. This section explores the concept of memory-mapped I/O and how it is implemented in assembly.

What is Memory-Mapped I/O?

In memory-mapped I/O, hardware devices are assigned memory addresses in the same address space as the CPU's memory. This allows the CPU to communicate with devices by reading from or writing to specific memory addresses, just like it does with RAM.

Memory-Mapped Registers

Devices connected via memory-mapped I/O typically expose their control and status registers as memory-mapped registers. These registers can be read and written to control the device's operation and retrieve information about its status.

For example, consider a simple I/O device that has a control register at memory address 0x1000 and a status register at address 0x1004. To enable the device, you might write a value to the control register:

```
mov eax, 0x1000    ; Address of the control register
mov ebx, 1         ; Value to enable the device
mov [eax], ebx     ; Write the value to the control register
```

And to check the status of the device, you can read from the status register:

```
mov eax, 0x1004    ; Address of the status register
mov ebx, [eax]     ; Read the status into EBX
```

Benefits of Memory-Mapped I/O

Memory-mapped I/O simplifies hardware interaction in assembly programming:

1. **Uniform Access:** Memory-mapped devices are accessed like memory, making I/O operations consistent with memory read and write operations.

2. **Efficiency:** Accessing memory-mapped registers is typically faster than using I/O ports, which require dedicated I/O instructions.

3. **Simplified Code:** Memory-mapped I/O reduces the need for complex I/O instructions and port addresses.

Memory-Mapped I/O in x86 Assembly

In x86 assembly, memory-mapped I/O can be implemented by accessing memory addresses as shown in the previous examples. However, some special instructions, like `in` and `out`, are also available for I/O operations.

Here's an example of using the `in` and `out` instructions to perform input and output operations on memory-mapped I/O ports:

```
; Output to port 0x1000
mov dx, 0x1000    ; Port address
mov al, 42        ; Data to send
out dx, al        ; Output to the port

; Input from port 0x1004
mov dx, 0x1004    ; Port address
in al, dx         ; Input from the port
```

Memory-Mapped I/O vs. Port-Mapped I/O

In addition to memory-mapped I/O, assembly languages may also support port-mapped I/O, where devices are accessed through specific I/O port addresses. The choice between memory-mapped and port-mapped I/O depends on the architecture and device.

Conclusion

Memory-mapped I/O is a powerful technique in assembly programming for interacting with hardware devices by treating them as memory locations. It simplifies device control, enhances code efficiency, and provides a consistent interface for accessing hardware resources. Understanding how to work with memory-mapped registers is essential when working with embedded systems and device drivers in assembly.

Section 5.5: Memory Protection and Segmentation

Memory protection and segmentation are essential concepts in assembly language programming, particularly when dealing with operating systems and multitasking environments. This section explores the significance of memory protection and segmentation and how they are managed in assembly.

Memory Protection

Memory protection is a crucial feature of modern operating systems that ensures the isolation and security of processes and prevents unauthorized access to memory regions. Memory protection mechanisms prevent one process from accessing or modifying the memory of another process, which is essential for maintaining system stability and security.

In assembly programming, memory protection is often implemented through hardware features, such as CPU privilege levels and page tables. These mechanisms restrict certain memory regions from being accessed or modified by user-level programs, ensuring that critical system data and code remain protected.

Segmentation

Segmentation is a memory management technique that divides memory into different segments, each with its own set of attributes and permissions. Segmentation allows fine-grained control over memory access by specifying access rights for each segment. Common attributes include read-only, read-write, execute, and no access.

In x86 assembly, segmentation is achieved using segment registers such as CS (Code Segment), DS (Data Segment), SS (Stack Segment), and ES (Extra Segment). Segment selectors are used to point to specific segments in the Global Descriptor Table (GDT) or Local Descriptor Table (LDT).

Here's an example of loading data from a segment using the DS register:

```
mov ax, 0x10        ; Load the segment selector for the data segment
mov ds, ax          ; Set the DS register to point to the data segment
mov ebx, [0x1234]   ; Load data from the data segment
```

Segmentation helps protect memory regions by controlling which segments can be accessed by which processes. It also enables efficient multitasking by isolating processes in their memory segments.

Paging

Paging is another memory management technique used in modern operating systems to provide virtual memory. Paging divides memory into fixed-size pages and allows processes to use a contiguous virtual address space while physical memory is managed in pages. Paging enables processes to have the illusion of a large address space, even when physical memory is limited.

In assembly, paging is typically managed through page tables, which map virtual addresses to physical addresses. The Memory Management Unit (MMU) handles the translation between virtual and physical addresses.

Memory Protection and Segmentation in Operating Systems

Operating systems play a significant role in managing memory protection and segmentation. They define memory protection policies, configure segment registers, and handle page table management to ensure the security and isolation of processes.

Assembly language programs running in user mode are subject to the memory protection mechanisms defined by the operating system. Attempts to access unauthorized memory regions will result in exceptions or segmentation faults.

Conclusion

Memory protection and segmentation are critical components of modern operating systems and are essential for maintaining system stability, security, and efficient memory management. Assembly language programmers working in operating system environments should be aware of these concepts and understand how to work within the memory protection boundaries established by the operating system.

Chapter 6: Input and Output Operations

Section 6.1: Accessing I/O Ports

In assembly language programming, one of the essential tasks is interacting with input and output (I/O) devices. This section explores how to access I/O ports directly from assembly code, a fundamental skill for tasks like device communication and hardware control.

I/O Ports in Assembly

I/O ports are hardware-level communication channels used by peripherals, such as keyboards, mice, displays, and more. These ports are a way for the CPU to exchange data with external devices. In assembly, you can access I/O ports using specialized instructions like in and out.

Using in and out Instructions

The in and out instructions are used to read from and write to I/O ports, respectively. They require two operands: the port number and the data register (usually al, ax, or eax) for data transfer.

Here's an example of reading a byte from port 0x60 (commonly used for keyboard input) into al:

```
in al, 0x60 ; Read a byte from port 0x60 into AL
```

And here's an example of writing a byte from al to port 0x3C8 (commonly used for color settings in graphics programming):

```
mov al, 0x0F  ; Set color index
out 0x3C8, al ; Write AL to port 0x3C8
```

Input and Output Operations

I/O operations can be essential in assembly programming, especially when dealing with devices directly. Common tasks include reading keyboard input, sending data to a display, or controlling external hardware. Understanding which ports to use and how to use them is crucial.

Port Addresses and Documentation

To perform I/O operations, you need to know the specific port addresses for the devices you're working with. This information can usually be found in hardware documentation or online resources provided by the device manufacturer.

Accessing I/O Ports Safely

While accessing I/O ports directly is a powerful capability, it must be done with caution. Incorrect or unauthorized access can lead to system instability or security vulnerabilities.

Therefore, when working with I/O ports, follow best practices and ensure that your code adheres to the expected behavior defined by the device's documentation.

Conclusion

Accessing I/O ports is a fundamental aspect of assembly language programming when interacting with hardware devices. Understanding how to use the in and out instructions and knowing the correct port addresses are essential skills for tasks involving device communication, control, and data exchange. Always exercise caution and follow documentation guidelines to ensure safe and effective I/O operations in your assembly programs.

Section 6.2: Console Input and Output

In assembly language programming, console input and output (I/O) operations are essential for interacting with users and displaying information on the screen. This section explores how to perform console I/O in assembly, which is a fundamental skill for creating text-based applications and debugging.

Console Output

Console output involves displaying information on the screen, such as messages, prompts, and results. In assembly, you can use the BIOS interrupt service routine (ISR) or direct video memory access for console output.

Using BIOS ISR

The BIOS ISR (Interrupt Service Routine) provides a set of functions for console output. The int 10h interrupt is commonly used for this purpose. Here's an example of how to use it to print a character to the screen:

```
mov ah, 0x0E ; Function code for teletype output
mov al, 'A'  ; Character to print
mov bh, 0x00 ; Page number (usually 0)
mov bl, 0x07 ; Text attribute (foreground color: white, background: black)
int 10h      ; Call BIOS ISR
```

Direct Video Memory Access

Alternatively, you can access video memory directly to display characters on the screen. Video memory starts at address 0xB8000 for color text mode. Here's an example of writing the character 'B' to the top-left corner of the screen:

```
mov edi, 0xB8000 ; Video memory address
mov byte [edi], 'B' ; Write 'B' character
```

Console Input

Console input involves reading user input from the keyboard. BIOS interrupts are commonly used for console input in assembly.

Using BIOS ISR

The int 16h interrupt is used for keyboard input. You can use it to wait for a key press and then retrieve the pressed key's scan code or ASCII value. Here's an example of waiting for a key press and storing the ASCII value in al:

```
mov ah, 0        ; Function code for keyboard input
int 16h          ; Call BIOS ISR
mov ah, 0x0E     ; Function code for teletype output
mov bh, 0x00     ; Page number (usually 0)
mov bl, 0x07     ; Text attribute (foreground color: white, background: black)
int 10h          ; Call BIOS ISR to echo the character
```

Input and Output Operations

Console I/O operations are crucial for creating interactive assembly programs and debugging code. They allow you to communicate with users and provide feedback. Understanding how to use BIOS interrupts or direct video memory access for console output and BIOS interrupts for console input is essential for building text-based applications.

Portability Considerations

When using BIOS interrupts for console I/O, it's important to note that these operations may not be portable across different operating systems or environments. BIOS functions are specific to the system's firmware and may not be available in all contexts. For cross-platform compatibility, consider using operating system-specific libraries or APIs for console I/O.

Conclusion

Console input and output are fundamental aspects of assembly language programming for creating interactive and user-friendly applications. Whether you choose to use BIOS interrupts or direct video memory access, mastering these techniques allows you to build text-based interfaces, receive user input, and provide feedback in your assembly programs.

Section 6.3: File Input and Output

File input and output (I/O) operations are vital in assembly language programming for tasks such as reading and writing files on disk. This section explores how to perform file I/O in assembly, a critical skill for handling data persistence and file manipulation.

File I/O involves reading data from files or writing data to files. In assembly, this is typically done using system calls provided by the operating system. These system calls allow your assembly program to interact with the file system.

Using System Calls

System calls are a standardized way for programs to request services from the operating system. In assembly, you can use system calls to perform file I/O operations. The exact system call numbers and calling conventions may vary depending on the operating system.

Here's an example of using the int 80h interrupt for file I/O in a Linux environment. This code opens a file, reads its contents, and then closes the file:

```
section .data
    filename db 'example.txt', 0    ; Null-terminated file name
    buf_size equ 1024               ; Buffer size for reading

section .bss
    fd resb 4                       ; File descriptor
    buffer resb buf_size            ; Buffer for file data
    bytes_read resb 4               ; Bytes read from file

section .text
    global _start

_start:
    ; Open the file for reading
    mov eax, 5                      ; System call number for open (5)
    mov ebx, filename               ; File name
    mov ecx, 0                      ; Flags (O_RDONLY)
    int 80h
    mov [fd], eax                   ; Store the file descriptor

    ; Read from the file
    mov eax, 3                      ; System call number for read (3)
    mov ebx, [fd]                   ; File descriptor
    mov ecx, buffer                 ; Buffer address
    mov edx, buf_size               ; Number of bytes to read
    int 80h
    mov [bytes_read], eax           ; Store the bytes read

    ; Close the file
    mov eax, 6                      ; System call number for close (6)
    mov ebx, [fd]                   ; File descriptor
    int 80h

    ; Exit
    mov eax, 1                      ; System call number for exit (1)
```

```
    xor ebx, ebx                    ; Exit code
    int 80h
```

When performing file I/O, it's crucial to handle errors properly. System calls typically return error codes in the eax register. You should check these error codes and take appropriate action in case of errors.

Portability Considerations

File I/O operations are highly dependent on the operating system and its specific system calls. Therefore, code that performs file I/O may not be portable across different operating systems. To ensure portability, you can use abstraction libraries or APIs provided by the operating system or development environment.

Conclusion

File input and output are essential aspects of assembly programming, allowing you to read and write data to and from files. By understanding how to use system calls and handle errors, you can implement file I/O operations in your assembly programs, enabling data persistence and file manipulation.

Section 6.4: Interfacing with Peripherals

Interfacing with peripherals is a crucial aspect of assembly language programming, especially when working with embedded systems or hardware control applications. This section explores how to communicate with various peripherals using assembly code.

Understanding Peripherals

Peripherals are external devices or hardware components that connect to a computer or microcontroller. Examples of peripherals include sensors, displays, input devices (such as keyboards and mice), and communication interfaces (such as UART, SPI, and I2C).

Communication Interfaces

To interface with peripherals, you need to understand the communication interfaces they use. Common interfaces include:

- **UART (Universal Asynchronous Receiver-Transmitter):** Used for serial communication between a microcontroller and external devices, such as GPS modules and Bluetooth modules.

- **SPI (Serial Peripheral Interface):** Used for synchronous serial communication between a microcontroller and devices like sensors, memory chips, and displays.

- **I2C (Inter-Integrated Circuit):** A two-wire communication protocol used for connecting microcontrollers to various sensors and devices.

- **GPIO (General-Purpose Input/Output):** Pins that can be configured as input or output and are often used for simple digital interfacing.

Accessing Peripherals

Accessing peripherals typically involves configuring the communication interface, sending or receiving data, and handling any necessary control signals. Let's take UART communication as an example:

```
section .data
    baud_rate equ 9600    ; UART baud rate
    uart_data db 0        ; Data to transmit

section .text
    global _start

_start:
    ; Configure UART communication
    mov al, 0x80          ; Enable divisor latch (DLAB)
    out 0x3F8, al         ; Set the UART control register
    mov al, 0x03          ; Set divisor low byte (115200 baud rate)
    out 0x3F8 + 0, al
    mov al, 0x00          ; Set divisor high byte
    out 0x3F8 + 1, al
    mov al, 0x03          ; 8-bit data, no parity, one stop bit
    out 0x3F8 + 3, al
    mov al, 0x01          ; Enable FIFOs
    out 0x3F8 + 2, al

    ; Send data via UART
    mov al, [uart_data]
    out 0x3F8, al

    ; Exit
    mov eax, 1            ; Exit syscall
    xor ebx, ebx          ; Exit code 0
    int 0x80
```

Peripheral Documentation

When working with peripherals, it's essential to consult their datasheets or documentation to understand their communication protocols, register configurations, and pin connections. Proper documentation ensures that you interface correctly and efficiently with the peripheral.

Interrupt-Driven I/O

In many cases, you can use interrupts for efficient and event-driven communication with peripherals. Interrupts allow your microcontroller or computer to respond to external events (e.g., data received via UART) without continuously polling the peripheral.

Conclusion

Interfacing with peripherals is a fundamental skill in assembly programming, especially when working on embedded systems or hardware control applications. Understanding the communication interfaces, configuring the necessary registers, and consulting peripheral documentation are essential steps in successfully interfacing with various external devices and sensors.

Section 6.5: Interrupt-Driven I/O

Interrupt-driven I/O is a powerful technique in assembly language programming that allows your program to respond to external events or inputs without continuous polling. This section explores the concept of interrupt-driven I/O and how it can be effectively implemented in assembly.

Understanding Interrupts

In the context of assembly programming, an interrupt is a signal to the processor that halts the execution of the current program to handle a specific event or condition. Interrupts can be generated by external hardware devices, such as a keyboard keypress, or they can be triggered by software.

Benefits of Interrupt-Driven I/O

Interrupt-driven I/O offers several advantages over polling-based I/O:

1. **Efficiency:** The CPU can focus on other tasks while waiting for an interrupt to occur, rather than continuously checking for a specific condition.

2. **Responsiveness:** The program can respond immediately to external events, reducing latency and ensuring timely processing.

3. **Simplicity:** Code that uses interrupts is often more straightforward and easier to maintain than polling-based code.

Implementation of Interrupt-Driven I/O

To implement interrupt-driven I/O, you typically follow these steps:

1. **Enable Interrupts:** Configure the interrupt controller to enable specific interrupt sources. For example, in x86 assembly, you might use the `sti` instruction to enable interrupts.

2. **Define an Interrupt Service Routine (ISR):** Write a dedicated ISR to handle the interrupt when it occurs. The ISR performs the necessary actions in response to the interrupt, such as reading data from a hardware device or updating program state.

3. **Link the ISR:** Connect the ISR to the interrupt source. This can involve configuring interrupt vectors or tables to map the interrupt source to the appropriate ISR.

4. **Clear the Interrupt:** After handling the interrupt in the ISR, clear the interrupt condition if necessary and restore the system to its previous state.

Example: Keyboard Input

Here's a simplified example of interrupt-driven keyboard input in x86 assembly:

```
section .data
    ; Define interrupt vector for keyboard (IRQ1)
    kb_interrupt equ 33

section .text
    global _start

_start:
    ; Enable interrupts
    sti

    ; Set up interrupt handler for keyboard
    mov edx, isr_keyboard
    mov eax, kb_interrupt
    call set_interrupt_handler

    ; Main program loop
    main_loop:
        ; Your program logic here

    ; Exit
    exit:
        ; Cleanup and exit code

; Interrupt Service Routine (ISR) for keyboard
isr_keyboard:
    ; Handle keyboard input
    ; Your code to process keyboard input here

    ; Notify the PIC (Programmable Interrupt Controller) that the interrupt i
s handled
    mov al, 0x20
    out 0x20, al
    ret
```

```
; Function to set an interrupt handler
set_interrupt_handler:
    ; Set up interrupt descriptor in IDT (Interrupt Descriptor Table)
    ; Your code to configure the IDT here

    ret
```

Conclusion

Interrupt-driven I/O is a fundamental technique in assembly programming for handling external events efficiently and responsively. By enabling interrupts, defining dedicated ISR handlers, and linking them to specific interrupt sources, you can create assembly programs that respond to hardware events, such as keyboard input, in a highly efficient and responsive manner.

Chapter 7: Assembly Language Debugging

Section 7.1: Debugging Tools and Techniques

Debugging is a critical part of the software development process, including assembly language programming. This section explores various debugging tools and techniques commonly used to identify and fix issues in assembly code.

The Importance of Debugging

Debugging is the process of identifying and correcting errors or issues in your code. In assembly programming, debugging is particularly essential due to the low-level nature of the code, making it more challenging to spot and fix problems.

Common Debugging Tools

1. *Interactive Debuggers:* Debuggers like GDB (GNU Debugger) provide a powerful environment for stepping through code, setting breakpoints, inspecting registers and memory, and analyzing program state.

2. *Print Statements:* Printing values or messages to the console is a basic but effective debugging technique. You can use assembly instructions like mov and int 80h in x86 assembly to print data.

```
section .data
    message db 'Debugging message', 0

section .text
    global _start

_start:
    ; Print a message
    mov eax, 4
    mov ebx, 1
    mov ecx, message
    mov edx, 18
    int 80h

    ; Your code here

    ; Exit
    mov eax, 1
    xor ebx, ebx
    int 80h
```

3. **Memory Dump:** *Examining memory contents can help identify data corruption or unexpected values. Debuggers often provide memory inspection capabilities.*

4. **Profiling Tools:** *Profilers can analyze the performance of your assembly code, helping you identify bottlenecks and optimize critical sections.*

5. **Tracing and Logging:** *Adding trace logs to your code can provide insight into the flow of execution and the values of variables at different points.*

Debugging Techniques

1. **Breakpoints:** *Setting breakpoints at specific code locations allows you to pause execution and inspect the program state. You can set breakpoints using debugger commands or by inserting software breakpoints (e.g., int 3 in x86 assembly).*

2. **Stepping:** *Stepping through code instruction by instruction helps you understand the flow and behavior of your program. Debuggers provide step-in, step-over, and step-out functionality.*

3. **Conditional Breakpoints:** *You can set breakpoints that trigger only when specific conditions are met. This is helpful for debugging complex logic.*

4. **Watchpoints:** *Watchpoints allow you to monitor changes to specific memory locations or variables, helping you identify when and where data is modified unexpectedly.*

Debugging Challenges

Debugging assembly code can be challenging due to factors like lack of high-level abstractions, limited debugging tools for specific architectures, and complex memory interactions. However, with practice and the right techniques, you can effectively debug assembly programs and ensure their correctness and reliability.

Conclusion

Debugging is an integral part of assembly language programming. Understanding the available debugging tools and techniques and practicing their use is crucial for identifying and resolving issues in your assembly code. Whether you're using interactive debuggers, print statements, or other methods, a systematic approach to debugging will help you create robust and error-free assembly programs.

Section 7.2: Code Profiling and Optimization

Code profiling and optimization are crucial steps in assembly language programming to ensure that your code runs efficiently and performs well. This section explores the concepts of profiling and optimization and how they apply to assembly code.

Understanding Code Profiling

Profiling is the process of analyzing a program's execution to identify performance bottlenecks, resource usage, and areas where optimization is needed. Profiling tools help you collect data on how your assembly code is executed, including details like the number of CPU cycles, memory usage, and function call statistics.

Profiling Tools

Several profiling tools are available for assembly language programming, depending on the target platform and architecture. Some common tools include:

*1. **Gprof:** Gprof is a profiling tool for GNU Compiler Collection (GCC) programs. While it primarily works with C and C++ code, you can also use it to profile assembly functions called from C/C++.*

*2. **Perf:** Perf is a Linux performance analysis tool that provides detailed information about CPU and memory usage. It can profile assembly code at a low level and is especially useful for optimizing system-level code.*

*3. **Valgrind:** Valgrind is a powerful instrumentation framework for memory profiling, debugging, and leak detection. It works with various languages, including assembly, and can help identify memory-related issues.*

Profiling Assembly Code

Profiling assembly code often involves adding markers or instrumentation points to your code to collect data during execution. These markers can include:

- **Function entry and exit points:** Measure the time spent in each function.

- **Loop counters:** Count the number of times loops are executed.

- **Memory access counters:** Track read and write operations to specific memory locations.

- **Resource usage counters:** Monitor resource allocation and usage.

Here's an example of adding profiling markers to assembly code:

```
section .text
    global _start

_start:
    ; Start profiling
    call start_profiling

    ; Your code here

    ; End profiling
    call end_profiling
```

```
    ; Exit
    mov eax, 1
    xor ebx, ebx
    int 80h

start_profiling:
    ; Start profiling code here
    ret

end_profiling:
    ; End profiling code here
    ret
```

Analyzing Profiling Data

Once you've collected profiling data, you can use the profiling tool of your choice to analyze the results. The output typically includes information on the most time-consuming functions, memory usage, and other performance metrics.

Optimization Strategies

Based on profiling data, you can identify performance bottlenecks and apply optimization strategies to improve your code's efficiency. Common optimization techniques for assembly code include:

- **Loop unrolling:** Expanding loops to reduce loop overhead.

- **Instruction scheduling:** Rearranging instructions to maximize pipelining and minimize stalls.

- **Register allocation:** Efficiently managing registers to reduce memory access.

- **Memory access optimization:** Minimizing memory reads and writes through caching and better data organization.

- **Parallelization:** Utilizing parallel processing and SIMD (Single Instruction, Multiple Data) instructions for vectorized operations.

Conclusion

Code profiling and optimization are essential steps in assembly language programming to ensure that your code performs efficiently and meets performance requirements. By using profiling tools, analyzing profiling data, and applying optimization strategies, you can enhance the speed and resource usage of your assembly programs, making them more effective and responsive.

Section 7.3: Tracing and Breakpoints

Tracing and breakpoints are fundamental debugging techniques that allow assembly language programmers to gain insight into the execution flow of their code and pause execution at specific points for inspection. This section delves into tracing and breakpoints and how they are employed in assembly debugging.

Tracing Execution

Tracing involves monitoring and recording the execution of an assembly program. This can be done by adding trace statements or logging information at critical points in the code. Tracing is valuable for understanding the program's behavior, identifying the sequence of executed instructions, and pinpointing issues or unexpected behavior.

Here's an example of adding trace statements in x86 assembly:

```
section .data
    trace_msg db 'Reached this point', 0

section .text
    global _start

_start:
    ; Your code here

    ; Add a trace message
    mov eax, 4
    mov ebx, 1
    mov ecx, trace_msg
    mov edx, 18
    int 80h

    ; Continue with your code

    ; Exit
    mov eax, 1
    xor ebx, ebx
    int 80h
```

In the example above, the program adds a trace message to the console, indicating when a specific point in the code is reached.

Using Breakpoints

Breakpoints are markers set within the code to halt program execution at a particular location. They are invaluable for examining the program state, registers, and memory when troubleshooting issues. Breakpoints can be set manually, either in code or through a debugging tool, and they allow you to interactively inspect variables and memory.

In x86 assembly, software breakpoints can be set using the `int 3` instruction. For example:

```
section .text
    global _start

_start:
    ; Your code here

    ; Set a software breakpoint
    int 3

    ; Continue with your code

    ; Exit
    mov eax, 1
    xor ebx, ebx
    int 80h
```

When the `int 3` instruction is encountered, it triggers an interrupt, and control is transferred to the debugger, allowing you to inspect the program's state.

Interactive Debuggers

Interactive debuggers like GDB (GNU Debugger) provide a comprehensive environment for setting breakpoints, stepping through code, and examining the program's execution. They allow you to control program flow, inspect registers and memory, and analyze variables interactively.

For example, in GDB, you can set breakpoints using the `break` command:

```
(gdb) break _start
```

This sets a breakpoint at the `_start` label, and when the program reaches that point, it halts execution, enabling you to investigate the program's state.

Conditional Breakpoints

Conditional breakpoints are breakpoints that trigger only when specific conditions are met. They are useful when you want to pause execution only when a certain condition is true. Debuggers allow you to set conditional breakpoints based on variables, registers, or other criteria.

```
(gdb) break function_name if variable_name == 0
```

In the example above, the breakpoint is set to halt execution at `function_name` only when `variable_name` equals zero.

Conclusion

Tracing and breakpoints are essential tools in the assembly language programmer's arsenal for debugging and troubleshooting. Tracing helps you monitor program execution and understand its behavior, while breakpoints allow you to pause execution at critical points for in-depth inspection. When used in conjunction with interactive debuggers, these techniques greatly facilitate the process of identifying and resolving issues in assembly code.

Section 7.4: Handling Exceptions and Errors

Handling exceptions and errors is a critical aspect of assembly language programming. In this section, we explore how assembly programs deal with exceptional situations and errors and the techniques used to manage them.

Exception Handling Mechanisms

Exception handling is the process of responding to exceptional conditions or events that occur during program execution. These exceptional conditions can include division by zero, invalid memory access, or unexpected external interrupts. In assembly language, exception handling typically involves the use of interrupt service routines (ISRs) and the Interrupt Descriptor Table (IDT).

1. **Interrupts and ISRs:** Interrupts are signals sent to the CPU to request its attention. When an exceptional condition occurs, the CPU can generate an interrupt, causing the execution to jump to a predefined ISR. Each exception type typically has a corresponding ISR to handle it.

2. **Interrupt Descriptor Table (IDT):** The IDT is a data structure that holds the addresses of ISR routines. When an interrupt occurs, the CPU consults the IDT to find the appropriate ISR and jumps to it.

Here's a simplified example of defining an ISR in x86 assembly for the divide-by-zero exception:

```
section .text

global isr0
isr0:
    ; Divide-by-zero exception handler
    ; Your code here

    ; End of ISR
    iret
```

Error handling in assembly language involves detecting and responding to runtime errors or conditions that may lead to unexpected program behavior or crashes. Common error-handling techniques include:

1. **Error Codes:** Functions or system calls often return error codes to indicate the success or failure of an operation. Assembly programs can check these error codes and take appropriate action.

2. **Error Messages:** Printing error messages to the console or log files can help developers diagnose issues. This is especially important for debugging and troubleshooting.

3. **Graceful Termination:** In the event of a severe error, it's essential to exit the program gracefully, releasing resources and ensuring that the system remains stable.

Debugging Exception Handling

Debugging exception handling code can be challenging due to its low-level nature and the potential for system instability. Interactive debuggers like GDB are valuable for stepping through ISR code, inspecting registers and memory, and diagnosing the cause of exceptions.

When debugging assembly code that includes exception handling, it's crucial to have a deep understanding of the target architecture's exception mechanisms and the specific ISRs associated with each exception type.

Exception Handling Best Practices

To effectively handle exceptions and errors in assembly programming, consider the following best practices:

- Thoroughly understand the architecture's exception and interrupt mechanisms.
- Properly initialize the IDT with the correct ISR addresses.
- Ensure that ISRs are written efficiently and do not introduce additional errors.
- Use error codes or status flags to communicate error conditions.
- Implement robust error messages and logging for debugging purposes.
- Test exception handling code under various scenarios to verify its correctness.

Conclusion

Handling exceptions and errors is a critical aspect of assembly language programming, as it ensures the robustness and reliability of your software. By implementing proper exception handling mechanisms, error detection, and graceful error recovery strategies, you can create assembly programs that are resilient and capable of responding to unexpected situations effectively. Debugging exception handling code is an essential skill for assembly programmers, as it allows you to diagnose and rectify issues that may compromise program stability and correctness.

Section 7.5: Debugging Real-World Scenarios

Debugging real-world assembly language programs often involves complex challenges and scenarios. In this section, we explore the intricacies of debugging assembly code in practical situations and provide insights into handling real-world debugging scenarios effectively.

Dealing with Optimization

Optimization is a common practice in assembly programming to enhance code performance. However, optimized code can be challenging to debug because the compiler may rearrange instructions, inline functions, or eliminate variables. When debugging optimized code, consider the following strategies:

- Disable optimization during development to ease debugging.
- Use debugging information generated by the compiler to map optimized code back to the original source code.
- Be aware that certain optimizations may affect variable values, making them appear different during debugging.

Multithreaded Debugging

Debugging multithreaded assembly programs adds complexity due to the potential for race conditions, deadlocks, and thread synchronization issues. Consider the following approaches for multithreaded debugging:

- Use thread-aware debuggers like GDB with multithreading support.
- Set breakpoints and examine variables within specific threads.
- Be cautious when modifying shared data during debugging, as it can impact the program's behavior.

Debugging Embedded Systems

Debugging assembly code on embedded systems presents unique challenges because of limited resources, absence of standard debugging tools, and real-time constraints. To debug embedded systems effectively:

- Employ in-circuit emulators (ICE) or hardware debuggers when available.
- Use serial or JTAG interfaces for remote debugging.
- Implement software-based debugging features in your embedded code, such as custom debug messages and status LEDs.

Debugging for Reverse Engineering

When debugging assembly code for reverse engineering purposes, such as analyzing malware or understanding proprietary software, it's essential to:

- Utilize disassemblers and debuggers tailored for reverse engineering tasks.
- Employ dynamic analysis techniques to observe program behavior in real-time.
- Study code execution patterns, memory allocations, and system interactions to gain insights.

Handling Complex Control Flow

Assembly code often features intricate control flow structures, including function pointers, indirect jumps, and conditional branches. Debugging such code requires:

- Setting breakpoints at critical decision points to analyze branching behavior.
- Using conditional breakpoints to halt execution only under specific conditions.
- Carefully examining register values and memory content to understand control flow decisions.

Debugging Interrupt Service Routines (ISRs)

Debugging ISRs, which are executed in response to hardware interrupts, can be challenging due to their asynchronous nature and limited debugging timeframes. To debug ISRs effectively:

- Use hardware debugging tools if available to capture real-time information during interrupts.
- Implement efficient logging mechanisms within ISRs to record critical data for later analysis.
- Employ software breakpoints sparingly, as they may disrupt interrupt-driven execution.

Conclusion

Debugging real-world assembly language programs requires a deep understanding of the target architecture, system constraints, and debugging tools. To navigate complex scenarios effectively, assembly programmers must adapt their debugging strategies to suit the specific challenges presented by optimization, multithreading, embedded systems, reverse engineering, complex control flow, and ISRs.

Successful debugging in these scenarios often relies on a combination of experience, creativity, and a solid understanding of assembly language principles. By mastering these skills, assembly programmers can effectively diagnose and resolve issues in diverse and challenging real-world environments.

Chapter 8: Assembly Language for System Programming

Section 8.1: Operating System Concepts

System programming in assembly language involves interfacing with an operating system to perform tasks like file I/O, memory management, and system calls. To understand this field, it's essential to grasp key operating system concepts. In this section, we explore these concepts and their relevance to assembly language system programming.

Operating System Basics

An operating system (OS) is system software that manages computer hardware and provides services to software applications. Key OS functions include process management, memory management, device management, file system management, and user interface support.

Processes and Threads

A process is an independent program in execution, complete with its own memory space and resources. A thread, on the other hand, is a unit of execution within a process. Understanding processes and threads is vital for system programming because interactions with the OS often involve managing processes and threads.

System Calls

System calls are interfaces provided by the OS that allow user-level programs to request services from the kernel. Common system calls include open, read, write, fork, exec, and exit. Assembly language programs can invoke these system calls to interact with the OS.

Here's an example of invoking the write system call in x86 assembly to print a message to the console:

```
section .data
    message db 'Hello, Assembly World!', 0

section .text
    global _start

_start:
    ; Prepare arguments for the write system call
    mov eax, 4          ; syscall number for write
    mov ebx, 1          ; file descriptor (stdout)
    mov ecx, message ; pointer to the message
    mov edx, 21         ; message length

    ; Invoke the write system call
    int 80h
```

```
; Exit
mov eax, 1
xor ebx, ebx
int 80h
```

Interrupts and Privilege Levels

Operating systems often use interrupts and privilege levels to enforce security and isolation. Understanding interrupt handling and privilege levels is crucial for assembly programmers who need to interact with the OS at the kernel level.

Synchronization and Concurrency

Synchronization and concurrency control mechanisms are essential for preventing race conditions and ensuring the safe execution of multiple processes or threads. Mutexes, semaphores, and condition variables are commonly used synchronization primitives in system programming.

Memory Management

Memory management involves allocating and deallocating memory dynamically, managing virtual memory, and handling memory protection. Understanding memory management concepts is vital when working with the OS to allocate and manipulate memory.

File Systems

File systems manage data storage and retrieval on storage devices. Assembly programmers may need to interact with the file system through system calls to read, write, and manipulate files.

Interacting with the OS

To interact with the OS effectively, assembly programmers must be familiar with the system's calling conventions, kernel APIs, and the specific requirements of the target OS. Additionally, system programming often involves handling errors and implementing error-checking mechanisms to ensure robustness.

Conclusion

Operating system concepts are fundamental to assembly language system programming. This knowledge provides the foundation for interfacing with the OS, invoking system calls, managing processes and threads, and performing a wide range of system-level tasks. As assembly programmers delve into system programming, they will apply these concepts to create efficient and reliable software that interacts seamlessly with the underlying operating system.

Section 8.2: Interrupt Handling

Interrupt handling is a fundamental aspect of system programming in assembly language. In this section, we delve into the concept of interrupts, their types, and how assembly language programs can manage and respond to interrupts effectively.

What Are Interrupts?

Interrupts are signals generated by hardware devices, timers, or other external sources that request the attention of the CPU. When an interrupt occurs, the CPU temporarily stops executing the current program and transfers control to a predefined interrupt handler or interrupt service routine (ISR). Interrupts allow the CPU to respond promptly to events without wasting processing cycles constantly checking for them.

Types of Interrupts

Interrupts can be categorized into several types, including:

1. **Hardware Interrupts:** These are generated by external hardware devices like keyboards, mice, disks, and network cards. Hardware interrupts are assigned specific interrupt numbers and corresponding ISRs.

2. **Software Interrupts:** Also known as system calls, software interrupts are generated by programs to request services from the operating system. Common examples include reading from files, writing to the console, or allocating memory.

3. **Exception Interrupts:** Exception interrupts occur in response to exceptional conditions, such as divide-by-zero errors, invalid memory access, or illegal instructions. Exception handling ISRs are crucial for maintaining system stability.

4. **Timer Interrupts:** Timer interrupts are generated by system timers and are often used for scheduling tasks, implementing multitasking, or maintaining system time.

Interrupt Descriptor Table (IDT)

The Interrupt Descriptor Table (IDT) is a data structure used by the CPU to map interrupt numbers to their corresponding ISRs. Assembly language programmers typically initialize the IDT to specify the memory addresses of ISRs for different interrupt types. Here's a simplified example of defining an ISR in x86 assembly and setting up the IDT:

```
section .text

global isr0
isr0:
    ; Divide-by-zero exception handler
    ; Your code here

    ; End of ISR
```

```
    iret

section .text

global idt_setup

idt_setup:
    lidt [idt_descriptor]
    ret

section .data

idt_descriptor:
    dw idt_end - idt_start - 1  ; IDT limit
    dd idt_start                ; IDT base

section .data

idt_start:
    dq isr0                     ; Divide-by-zero ISR address
    dq 0                        ; Reserved
    ; Add more ISR addresses for other interrupt types here
idt_end:
```

Interrupt Handling in Assembly

When an interrupt occurs, the CPU pushes the current context onto the stack, transfers control to the ISR, and pops the context back when the ISR is done. Assembly language ISRs typically follow a specific convention, such as saving and restoring registers, acknowledging the interrupt, and ending with an iret instruction to return to the interrupted program.

Enabling and Disabling Interrupts

In certain scenarios, it may be necessary to enable or disable interrupts. For example, during critical sections of code where data consistency is crucial, you may disable interrupts temporarily. On the other hand, enabling interrupts allows the system to respond to external events. In x86 assembly, the cli instruction disables interrupts, while sti enables them.

Debugging Interrupt Handling

Debugging interrupt handling code can be challenging due to its asynchronous nature. Interactive debuggers like GDB can be invaluable for setting breakpoints within ISRs, inspecting memory and registers, and tracking the flow of execution.

Conclusion

Interrupt handling is a fundamental concept in system programming with assembly language. By understanding the types of interrupts, initializing the Interrupt Descriptor Table (IDT), implementing ISRs, and managing interrupt enable/disable states, assembly programmers can effectively respond to hardware events and system calls, making their software more responsive and robust. Debugging interrupt handling code is an essential skill for system programmers, as it allows them to diagnose and rectify issues that may affect system stability and reliability.

Section 8.3: Device Drivers and Kernel Modules

Device drivers and kernel modules play a crucial role in system programming, allowing hardware devices to communicate with the operating system and user-level applications. In this section, we explore the concepts of device drivers and kernel modules, their significance, and how they are implemented in assembly language.

What Are Device Drivers?

Device drivers are software components that act as intermediaries between hardware devices and the operating system. They provide a standardized interface for the OS to communicate with different types of hardware, including peripherals, storage devices, network adapters, and more. Device drivers abstract the low-level details of hardware access, enabling the OS and user applications to interact with devices using a uniform API.

Kernel Modules

Kernel modules are pieces of code that can be dynamically loaded into the running kernel to extend its functionality. These modules can implement device drivers, file systems, and other kernel-level services. Kernel modules allow for the modular design of the kernel, enhancing its flexibility and maintainability.

Device Driver Development

Developing a device driver in assembly language involves several key steps:

1. **Initialization:** The driver initializes the hardware device it controls, configuring its settings and preparing it for use. This may include setting up registers, enabling interrupts, and allocating memory.

2. **Registration:** The driver registers itself with the operating system, informing the OS about the device it manages and the functions it provides.

3. **Interrupt Handling:** Device drivers often need to handle interrupts generated by the hardware device. The driver's interrupt service routine (ISR) responds to these interrupts, allowing the device to signal events or send data to the system.

4. **Data Transfer:** Device drivers facilitate data transfer between user applications and the hardware device. This includes reading data from sensors, writing data to storage devices, or transmitting data over a network.

5. **Error Handling:** Device drivers must handle errors gracefully, ensuring system stability even when hardware encounters issues. Error handling may involve recovering from errors, reporting them to the OS, or notifying user applications.

Kernel Module Development

Kernel modules are designed to be loaded and unloaded dynamically, making them a versatile way to extend kernel functionality. Developing a kernel module in assembly language involves the following steps:

1. **Initialization:** The module's initialization function is called when it is loaded into the kernel. This function sets up data structures, allocates resources, and prepares the module for operation.

2. **Registration:** Kernel modules often register themselves with the kernel, specifying the services they provide and any parameters they accept.

3. **Functionality:** The module implements specific functionality, which can range from device drivers to additional file systems, network protocols, or system services.

4. **Cleanup:** When the module is unloaded or during system shutdown, its cleanup function is called to release resources, unregister services, and perform any necessary cleanup tasks.

Debugging Device Drivers and Kernel Modules

Debugging device drivers and kernel modules can be challenging due to their privileged nature and interaction with hardware. Debugging tools like GDB can be used in conjunction with kernel debugging mechanisms to inspect memory, registers, and code execution within these modules.

Conclusion

Device drivers and kernel modules are critical components of modern operating systems, allowing them to support a wide range of hardware devices and extend their functionality. Understanding how to develop and debug these components in assembly language is essential for system programmers. Device drivers enable the efficient and standardized communication between hardware and software layers, while kernel modules offer a way to enhance kernel capabilities without requiring a full kernel rebuild. Mastering the development and debugging of device drivers and kernel modules empowers assembly language programmers to create robust and versatile system software.

Section 8.4: System Calls and API

System calls and Application Programming Interfaces (APIs) are essential aspects of system programming in assembly language. In this section, we explore the concepts of system calls, their significance, and how they are utilized to interact with the operating system and provide services to user-level applications.

Understanding System Calls

System calls are functions provided by the operating system's kernel that allow user-level programs to request services and perform privileged operations, such as file I/O, process management, memory allocation, and more. System calls act as a bridge between user space and kernel space, enabling secure and controlled interactions between application code and the operating system.

Common System Calls

Common system calls found in most operating systems include:

1. **File System Operations:** These system calls enable the creation, reading, writing, and manipulation of files and directories. Examples include open, read, write, close, and stat.

2. **Process Management:** System calls for process management allow applications to create, terminate, and manipulate processes. Examples include fork, exec, wait, and exit.

3. **Memory Management:** These system calls control memory allocation and deallocation. malloc, free, mmap, and brk are examples used for memory management.

4. **Input and Output:** System calls for I/O operations permit applications to interact with devices and files. read, write, ioctl, and select are commonly used for I/O.

5. **Interprocess Communication (IPC):** IPC system calls facilitate communication and data exchange between processes. Examples include pipe, shmget, and msgsend.

Using System Calls in Assembly

To invoke a system call in assembly language, you typically use a specific instruction or software interrupt that transfers control to a designated system call handler in the kernel. The exact mechanism may vary between architectures, but on x86, the int 0x80 instruction is commonly used for this purpose.

Here's a simplified example of how to use a system call in x86 assembly to write a string to the console:

```
section .data
    hello db 'Hello, world!',0
    len equ $ - hello

section .text
global _start

_start:
    ; Prepare syscall parameters
    mov eax, 4          ; sys_write
    mov ebx, 1          ; file descriptor (stdout)
    mov ecx, hello      ; pointer to the string
    mov edx, len        ; string length

    ; Invoke the syscall
    int 0x80

    ; Exit the program
    mov eax, 1          ; sys_exit
    xor ebx, ebx        ; exit code 0
    int 0x80
```

Kernel API

In addition to system calls, the kernel often provides an API that allows developers to access kernel functionality directly from user-level applications. This API comprises libraries and header files that define functions and data structures for interacting with the kernel. Developing kernel-level software in assembly language often involves utilizing this API to access low-level services and features.

Debugging System Calls and API Usage

Debugging assembly code that interacts with system calls and APIs can be challenging due to the interaction between user-level and kernel-level code. Debugging tools like GDB can help you trace the flow of execution, inspect memory, and diagnose issues in your assembly programs.

Conclusion

System calls and APIs are integral components of assembly language programming for systems and applications. Understanding how to use system calls to interact with the operating system, along with the kernel API for advanced functionality, is essential for building efficient and powerful software. Debugging tools and techniques are valuable assets when developing and maintaining assembly code that utilizes system calls and APIs, helping to ensure correct and reliable behavior of your programs.

Section 8.5: Building System Software in Assembly

Building system software in assembly language is a complex but rewarding endeavor. In this section, we delve into the challenges and benefits of writing system-level software in assembly, explore the use cases, and discuss best practices.

Challenges of System Software in Assembly

Writing system software in assembly poses several challenges:

1. **Portability:** Assembly code is highly architecture-dependent, making it less portable across different CPU architectures. This can limit the platform on which the software can run.

2. **Complexity:** System-level software often requires complex interactions with hardware and the operating system. Managing low-level details can be error-prone and challenging to debug.

3. **Maintenance:** Assembly code tends to be more challenging to maintain and extend over time, especially when dealing with evolving hardware and software environments.

4. **Security:** Writing secure system software is crucial, as vulnerabilities can lead to critical system failures or security breaches. Ensuring security in assembly code requires careful consideration of potential vulnerabilities and robust error handling.

Benefits of Assembly in System Software

Despite its challenges, assembly language offers several benefits for system-level programming:

1. **Performance:** Assembly code can be highly optimized for specific tasks and architectures, leading to efficient and fast system software.

2. **Low-Level Control:** Assembly provides precise control over hardware resources, allowing developers to fine-tune system software for optimal performance.

3. **Minimal Overhead:** Assembly code typically incurs minimal runtime overhead, making it suitable for real-time and resource-constrained systems.

4. **Kernel Development:** Writing kernel modules, device drivers, and other core system components often necessitates the use of assembly language to interact directly with hardware and the kernel.

Use Cases for Assembly in System Software

Assembly language is well-suited for various system-level tasks, including:

1. **Bootloaders:** Bootloaders are responsible for initializing the system and loading the operating system. Many bootloaders are written in assembly to minimize their size and execution time.

2. **Kernel Development:** Building operating system kernels and kernel modules often requires assembly code to manage hardware and implement critical functions.

3. **Device Drivers:** Writing efficient device drivers, especially for hardware with specific requirements, often involves assembly language to interact with the hardware directly.

4. **Embedded Systems:** Assembly is commonly used in embedded systems programming, where resource constraints and real-time requirements are prevalent.

5. **Legacy Systems:** Maintaining and extending legacy systems may require working with existing assembly codebases.

Best Practices for Assembly in System Software

When writing system software in assembly, consider the following best practices:

1. **Documentation:** Thoroughly document your code, including comments and explanations of critical sections and algorithms.

2. **Modularity:** Divide your code into well-defined modules and functions to improve readability and maintainability.

3. **Testing:** Rigorously test your code to identify and fix issues early in development.

4. **Optimization:** Focus on optimizing critical code paths for performance while maintaining readability and correctness in less critical sections.

5. **Security:** Prioritize security by carefully validating inputs, implementing robust error handling, and following secure coding practices.

6. **Compatibility:** Be mindful of platform-specific differences and consider portability and future-proofing when necessary.

In conclusion, building system software in assembly language can be a powerful choice when performance, low-level control, and resource efficiency are critical. However, it comes with challenges that require careful consideration, thorough testing, and adherence to best practices to ensure the reliability, security, and maintainability of your code.

Chapter 9: Assembly Language for Embedded Systems

Section 9.1: Introduction to Embedded Systems

Embedded systems are specialized computer systems designed to perform dedicated functions or tasks within a larger system. They are characterized by their integration into a specific device or product, where they control and manage hardware components to provide desired functionality. In this section, we'll explore the fundamentals of embedded systems and how assembly language plays a crucial role in their development.

What Are Embedded Systems?

Embedded systems are everywhere in our daily lives, often operating silently and efficiently behind the scenes. They can be found in a wide range of devices, including:

- **Consumer Electronics:** Smartphones, televisions, microwave ovens, and digital cameras all contain embedded systems.

- **Automotive:** Embedded systems control the engine, transmission, airbags, entertainment systems, and more in modern vehicles.

- **Industrial Automation:** Manufacturing processes, robotics, and control systems rely on embedded systems for precision and efficiency.

- **Medical Devices:** Devices like pacemakers, infusion pumps, and diagnostic equipment utilize embedded systems for critical functions.

- **IoT Devices:** Smart thermostats, wearable fitness trackers, and home automation devices are powered by embedded systems.

Characteristics of Embedded Systems

Embedded systems differ from general-purpose computers in several ways:

1. **Dedicated Functionality:** Embedded systems are designed for specific tasks, often with a singular purpose. They don't have the versatility of general-purpose computers.

2. **Resource Constraints:** These systems are often resource-constrained, with limited memory, processing power, and storage capacity. Efficient code is essential.

3. **Real-Time Operation:** Many embedded systems operate in real-time, meaning they must respond to inputs or events within strict timing constraints.

4. **Reliability:** Embedded systems are expected to work reliably for extended periods, even in harsh environments.

5. **Low Power:** Power efficiency is crucial, especially for battery-powered devices and IoT applications.

Role of Assembly Language in Embedded Systems

Assembly language is a valuable tool for embedded systems development due to its low-level control and efficiency. Here's why assembly language is commonly used in embedded systems:

- **Precise Hardware Control:** Assembly language allows developers to access and control hardware directly, which is vital in embedded systems where efficiency and fine-grained control are essential.

- **Efficiency:** Assembly code can be highly optimized for a specific target architecture, making it more efficient in terms of speed and resource utilization compared to high-level languages.

- **Real-Time Capabilities:** For real-time embedded systems, assembly language is often the preferred choice as it enables developers to meet strict timing requirements.

- **Resource Management:** Embedded systems often have limited resources. Assembly code allows developers to manage these resources efficiently, including memory, I/O, and power.

- **Portability:** Assembly code can be adapted for different microcontroller architectures, providing a degree of portability for embedded projects.

Example of Assembly in Embedded Systems

Consider a simple embedded system task: controlling an LED display on a microcontroller. Assembly language allows you to precisely control the pins connected to the LEDs, set their states, and implement timing for blinking patterns. Here's a simplified example in x86 assembly (note that real embedded systems typically use microcontroller-specific assembly languages):

```
section .data
    led_port equ 0x1000   ; Memory-mapped I/O port for LED control

section .text
global _start

_start:
    mov eax, 0x1        ; Set EAX to turn on LED
    out led_port, eax   ; Write to the I/O port to control the LED

    ; Add delay here for blinking pattern

    mov eax, 0x0        ; Set EAX to turn off LED
    out led_port, eax   ; Write to the I/O port to turn off the LED
```

```
; Add another delay for the pattern

; Repeat the pattern or enter a loop for continuous operation

; Exit the program or loop indefinitely
```

In this example, assembly language allows you to interact directly with the LED hardware, set its state, and implement timing for the blinking pattern, showcasing the level of control assembly provides in embedded systems.

Conclusion

Embedded systems are a pervasive part of our modern world, driving numerous devices and applications. Assembly language is a powerful tool for developing embedded system software due to its precise control, efficiency, and suitability for resource-constrained environments. Understanding assembly language is crucial for embedded systems developers to create efficient, reliable, and real-time systems that meet the specific requirements of their applications. In the subsequent sections of this chapter, we will delve deeper into microcontrollers, firmware development, real-time operating systems, and practical examples of embedded applications in assembly language.

Section 9.2: Microcontrollers and Microprocessors

Microcontrollers and microprocessors are fundamental components in the world of embedded systems. In this section, we'll explore the differences between these two key elements and their roles in embedded system design.

Microcontrollers

Microcontrollers are compact, self-contained computing devices that integrate a microprocessor, memory, input/output peripherals, and often, specialized hardware components on a single chip. They are designed for specific tasks and are commonly used in embedded systems due to their efficiency and low cost.

Key characteristics of microcontrollers include:

- **Integrated Components:** Microcontrollers typically include essential components like central processing units (CPUs), memory (both program and data memory), timers, and I/O ports on a single chip.

- **Low Power Consumption:** Microcontrollers are designed to operate efficiently on minimal power, making them suitable for battery-powered and energy-efficient applications.

- **Real-Time Processing:** Many microcontrollers are optimized for real-time processing, allowing them to respond to external events with low latency.

- **Application-Specific:** Microcontrollers are tailored to specific applications, such as automotive control, home automation, and IoT devices.

- **Limited Processing Power:** While microcontrollers are powerful for their intended tasks, they usually have lower processing power compared to microprocessors.

Microprocessors

Microprocessors, on the other hand, are the central processing units (CPUs) found in general-purpose computers and devices. They lack the integrated peripherals and hardware components found in microcontrollers. Instead, microprocessors are part of a larger system and rely on external components, such as memory, input/output devices, and peripherals.

Key characteristics of microprocessors include:

- **General-Purpose:** Microprocessors are designed for general-purpose computing and can run a wide range of software applications, from operating systems to user applications.

- **Higher Processing Power:** Microprocessors are more powerful in terms of processing capabilities compared to microcontrollers, making them suitable for complex tasks.

- **External Components:** Microprocessors require external components like RAM, ROM, and peripheral interfaces to function effectively.

- **Less Energy-Efficient:** Due to their higher processing power and external dependencies, microprocessors tend to consume more power compared to microcontrollers.

Choosing Between Microcontrollers and Microprocessors

The choice between using a microcontroller or microprocessor in an embedded system depends on the specific requirements of the application. Here are some considerations:

- **Task Complexity:** For simple, dedicated tasks with real-time requirements, microcontrollers are often a better choice due to their integrated hardware and low power consumption.

- **Processing Power:** If the application requires significant computational power, a microprocessor may be more appropriate, as it can handle more complex tasks and run a wider range of software.

- **Cost:** Microcontrollers are typically more cost-effective, making them suitable for applications with budget constraints.

- **Energy Efficiency:** Microcontrollers excel in energy-efficient applications, making them ideal for battery-powered devices and IoT applications.

- **Flexibility:** Microprocessors offer greater flexibility, allowing developers to run a variety of software, making them suitable for versatile applications.

Here are examples of scenarios where microcontrollers and microprocessors are commonly used:

- **Microcontroller:** A temperature control system for a household thermostat uses a microcontroller to read temperature sensors, control heating or cooling, and display information on an LED screen.

- **Microprocessor:** A smartphone uses a microprocessor to run the operating system, execute applications, and provide a wide range of user functionalities.

Understanding the differences between microcontrollers and microprocessors is crucial when designing embedded systems. The choice of hardware significantly impacts the performance, power consumption, and capabilities of the embedded device, and it should align with the specific requirements of the application. In the following sections, we'll delve deeper into firmware development for microcontrollers and explore real-time operating systems for embedded systems development.

Section 9.3: Firmware Development

Firmware is a critical component of embedded systems, serving as the software that runs on microcontrollers and microprocessors. In this section, we'll explore the process of firmware development, the tools commonly used, and best practices for creating reliable and efficient firmware.

Understanding Firmware

Firmware refers to software that is permanently or semi-permanently stored in a device's non-volatile memory. It is responsible for controlling the device's hardware components, responding to external inputs, and executing specific tasks. Unlike traditional software, firmware is closely tied to the hardware it runs on and is essential for the proper functioning of embedded systems.

The Firmware Development Process

Firmware development typically follows a structured process that includes the following stages:

1. **Requirements Analysis:** The first step involves understanding the functional requirements of the embedded system. What tasks must the firmware perform? What hardware components will it interact with? This stage sets the foundation for the firmware design.

2. **Firmware Design:** Based on the requirements, firmware designers create a high-level design of the software architecture. This includes defining the structure of the firmware, the flow of data, and the algorithms used.

3. **Coding:** Once the design is complete, developers write the firmware code using programming languages suitable for the target microcontroller or microprocessor. Common languages include C and C++.

4. **Compilation:** The source code is then compiled into machine code that can be executed by the microcontroller or microprocessor. The compiler used depends on the specific architecture and platform.

5. **Testing and Debugging:** Rigorous testing is crucial to ensure the firmware works as intended. Testing may include unit testing, integration testing, and real-world testing on the target hardware. Debugging tools are essential for identifying and resolving issues.

6. **Optimization:** Firmware developers often need to optimize code for performance and resource efficiency. This is critical, especially in resource-constrained embedded systems.

7. **Documentation:** Proper documentation of the firmware code and its functionality is essential for future maintenance and troubleshooting.

8. **Deployment:** Once the firmware is thoroughly tested and optimized, it is deployed to the target microcontroller or microprocessor. This can be done via programming tools, bootloaders, or other methods.

Tools for Firmware Development

Several tools and software development environments are commonly used in firmware development:

*   **Integrated Development Environments (IDEs):** IDEs like Keil, MPLAB X, and PlatformIO provide a complete development environment with code editors, compilers, debuggers, and simulation capabilities.

*   **Compilers:** Compilers such as GCC (GNU Compiler Collection) and specific microcontroller manufacturer compilers are used to convert high-level code into machine code.

*   **Debugging Tools:** Debugging tools like JTAG debuggers, in-circuit emulators (ICE), and serial debuggers help identify and fix issues in the firmware.

*   **Simulators:** Some IDEs and development environments offer simulation capabilities, allowing developers to test firmware without the physical hardware.

To ensure the reliability and maintainability of firmware, developers should follow these best practices:

- **Modularity:** Divide firmware into modular components to simplify development and maintenance.

- **Version Control:** Use version control systems like Git to track changes and collaborate with other developers.

- **Code Reviews:** Conduct code reviews to identify issues and ensure code quality.

- **Error Handling:** Implement robust error handling mechanisms to handle unexpected situations gracefully.

- **Resource Management:** Manage resources like memory and peripherals efficiently to avoid resource conflicts.

- **Documentation:** Document code, including comments and user guides, for clear understanding and future reference.

- **Security:** Incorporate security measures to protect the firmware from vulnerabilities and attacks.

Firmware development is a critical aspect of embedded systems design, and a well-structured development process, the right tools, and adherence to best practices are essential for creating reliable and efficient firmware for microcontrollers and microprocessors. In the next section, we will explore real-time operating systems (RTOS) commonly used in embedded systems to manage tasks and resources efficiently.

Section 9.4: Real-Time Operating Systems (RTOS)

Real-time operating systems (RTOS) are essential components in many embedded systems, providing a framework for managing tasks, scheduling, and resource allocation. In this section, we will delve into the significance of RTOS in embedded systems, their architecture, and how they streamline the development of complex embedded applications.

The Role of RTOS in Embedded Systems

Embedded systems often require precise timing and efficient management of resources. RTOS is designed to meet these requirements by offering the following key features:

1. **Task Scheduling:** RTOS allows you to define tasks or threads that can run concurrently. It employs scheduling algorithms to determine which task should execute next, ensuring that critical tasks are prioritized.

2. **Deterministic Timing:** In real-time applications, meeting deadlines is crucial. RTOS provides deterministic timing, ensuring that tasks are executed within predefined time constraints.

3. **Resource Management:** Embedded systems often have limited resources like memory and peripherals. RTOS efficiently manages these resources, preventing conflicts and ensuring optimal utilization.

4. **Interrupt Handling:** RTOS handles hardware and software interrupts, allowing the system to respond to external events promptly.

5. **Inter-Task Communication:** RTOS provides mechanisms for tasks to communicate with each other, such as message queues, semaphores, and shared memory.

RTOS Architecture

The architecture of an RTOS typically includes the following components:

1. **Kernel:** The kernel is the core of the RTOS responsible for task scheduling, resource management, and interrupt handling. It provides the essential services required for real-time operation.

2. **Task Management:** RTOS manages multiple tasks or threads. Each task has its own context, including stack, registers, and program counter. Task management includes task creation, deletion, and switching.

3. **Interrupt Handling:** Hardware and software interrupts are handled by the RTOS to ensure timely response to external events. Interrupt service routines (ISRs) are part of this component.

4. **Scheduler:** The scheduler is responsible for determining the order in which tasks run. It employs scheduling algorithms like priority-based scheduling, round-robin scheduling, or rate-monotonic scheduling.

5. **Timers:** Timers are essential for tracking time intervals and managing timeouts. RTOS provides mechanisms for setting and handling timers.

6. **Inter-Task Communication:** RTOS offers various inter-task communication mechanisms, including message queues, semaphores, and mutexes, allowing tasks to share data and synchronize their execution.

Popular RTOS for Embedded Systems

There are several RTOS options available for embedded systems, each with its strengths and suitability for different applications:

- **FreeRTOS:** FreeRTOS is a popular open-source RTOS known for its small footprint and wide adoption in various embedded projects.

- **Micrium μC/OS:** μC/OS is a commercial RTOS with a scalable architecture and support for different microcontrollers and processors.

- **VxWorks:** VxWorks is a commercial RTOS known for its reliability and real-time capabilities, commonly used in industries like aerospace and automotive.

- **QNX:** QNX is a POSIX-compliant RTOS used in safety-critical applications, including medical devices and automotive systems.

Benefits of Using RTOS in Embedded Systems

The adoption of RTOS in embedded systems offers several benefits:

1. **Deterministic Behavior:** RTOS ensures that tasks meet deadlines consistently, making it suitable for real-time applications like automotive control systems and industrial automation.

2. **Efficient Resource Management:** RTOS optimizes resource usage, allowing embedded systems to operate efficiently even with limited resources.

3. **Modularity:** RTOS encourages a modular software design, making it easier to maintain and update embedded applications.

4. **Interoperability:** RTOS supports communication between tasks and devices, enabling seamless integration of various components.

5. **Scalability:** Many RTOS options are scalable, allowing them to adapt to the needs of both small and large embedded systems.

In summary, real-time operating systems play a pivotal role in the development of embedded systems, ensuring reliable and deterministic operation. They offer essential features like task scheduling, resource management, and inter-task communication, making them indispensable tools for embedded system developers. In the next section, we will explore the world of IoT and its relevance to assembly language programming in embedded systems.

Section 9.5: Developing IoT Solutions in Assembly

The Internet of Things (IoT) is a rapidly growing field that involves connecting everyday objects to the internet, allowing them to collect and exchange data. IoT has a significant impact on various industries, from smart homes and healthcare to industrial automation and agriculture. In this section, we'll explore the role of assembly language in developing IoT solutions and the unique challenges it presents.

While high-level languages like C and Python are commonly used for IoT development due to their ease of programming, there are scenarios where assembly language becomes relevant:

1. **Resource-Constrained Devices:** IoT devices often have limited processing power and memory. Assembly language can be used to write efficient and compact code that maximizes resource utilization.

2. **Low-Level Hardware Access:** IoT applications sometimes require direct access to hardware components like sensors and communication modules. Assembly allows for precise control over hardware interfaces.

3. **Real-Time Requirements:** Some IoT applications demand real-time responses, such as industrial control systems and robotics. Assembly can provide the deterministic timing required for these applications.

4. **Customization:** Assembly language allows developers to create highly specialized code tailored to specific IoT devices or applications, optimizing performance and power consumption.

Challenges of IoT Development in Assembly

Developing IoT solutions in assembly language comes with its set of challenges:

1. **Steep Learning Curve:** Assembly language is more complex than high-level languages, requiring developers to have a deep understanding of hardware architecture.

2. **Portability:** Assembly code written for one processor may not work on another, making it less portable compared to higher-level languages.

3. **Debugging and Maintenance:** Debugging assembly code can be challenging, and maintaining it over time may require more effort than higher-level languages.

4. **Time-to-Market:** IoT projects often have tight development schedules. Writing code in assembly language may extend development time, which can be a disadvantage in competitive markets.

Use Cases for Assembly in IoT

Despite the challenges, there are specific use cases where assembly language can shine in IoT development:

1. **Sensor Data Processing:** IoT devices often collect data from various sensors. Assembly can efficiently process sensor data and perform necessary calculations with minimal overhead.

2. **Custom Communication Protocols:** When working with specialized communication protocols or low-level interfaces, assembly can provide precise control over data transmission and reception.

3. **Battery-Powered Devices:** For battery-powered IoT devices, optimizing power consumption is critical. Assembly code can be tailored to minimize energy consumption during device operation.

Assembly Language and IoT Frameworks

IoT development often leverages IoT frameworks and platforms that provide higher-level abstractions for device management and communication. While these frameworks are typically designed for higher-level languages, it's possible to integrate assembly code for specific performance-critical tasks.

For example, in an IoT device running on a microcontroller, you might use a C-based IoT framework for most of the application logic, but you could implement time-critical tasks or hardware-specific operations in assembly language modules.

Conclusion

In the realm of IoT, assembly language has a niche but essential role to play. It is best suited for situations where resource optimization, low-level hardware control, and real-time performance are paramount. While the majority of IoT development is done in higher-level languages, knowing when and how to leverage assembly language can be a valuable skill for IoT developers working on resource-constrained or performance-critical projects. In the following chapters, we will explore assembly's application in various domains, including reverse engineering, game development, and multimedia processing.

Chapter 10: Assembly Language for Reverse Engineering

Section 10.1: Reverse Engineering Fundamentals

Reverse engineering is a process of dissecting and understanding how a software or hardware system works, often without access to its original source code or documentation. This practice is crucial in various domains, including security analysis, software maintenance, and product improvement. In this section, we will delve into the fundamentals of reverse engineering and explore how assembly language plays a vital role in this process.

Why Reverse Engineering?

1. **Understanding Legacy Systems:** Legacy software or hardware systems might lack proper documentation or have outdated codebases. Reverse engineering allows engineers to comprehend and extend these systems.

2. **Security Analysis:** Security researchers use reverse engineering to discover vulnerabilities in software and hardware, leading to more secure systems.

3. **Interoperability:** Reverse engineering enables the development of compatible software or hardware components that can interact with proprietary systems.

4. **Malware Analysis:** Reverse engineers dissect malware to understand its behavior, helping in the development of countermeasures.

The Role of Assembly Language

Assembly language is a fundamental tool in reverse engineering for several reasons:

- **Low-Level Understanding:** Assembly provides a low-level view of how a system operates, making it suitable for dissecting machine code and binary formats.

- **Disassembly:** Reverse engineers often start by disassembling executable binaries into assembly code, making it human-readable and easier to analyze.

- **Reconstruction:** Assembly code can be used to reconstruct high-level code or hardware designs, aiding in understanding and potentially modifying the system.

Tools for Reverse Engineering

Several tools are commonly used in reverse engineering:

1. **Disassemblers:** Software tools that convert machine code or executables into human-readable assembly code. Examples include IDA Pro and Ghidra.

2. **Debuggers:** Tools that allow reverse engineers to step through code, set breakpoints, and inspect memory during program execution. GDB is a popular debugger.

3. **Hex Editors:** These tools enable manual inspection and modification of binary files at the hexadecimal level.

4. **Decompilers:** For high-level code reconstruction, decompilers attempt to convert assembly code back into a higher-level language, such as C or C++.

Reverse Engineering Methodology

The reverse engineering process typically involves the following steps:

1. **Data Collection:** Gather all available information about the system, including binaries, documentation, and any relevant data.

2. **Static Analysis:** Analyze the system without running it, often involving disassembly and code inspection.

3. **Dynamic Analysis:** Execute the system in a controlled environment, monitoring its behavior and interactions.

4. **Pattern Recognition:** Identify common structures, algorithms, and patterns in the code.

5. **Documentation:** Document the findings, including the system's architecture, algorithms, and vulnerabilities.

Legal and Ethical Considerations

It's essential to be aware of legal and ethical considerations when engaging in reverse engineering. Depending on your jurisdiction and the specific context, reverse engineering might involve intellectual property issues or run afoul of terms of service agreements. Always consider the legal and ethical implications of your actions.

Conclusion

Reverse engineering is a valuable skill for understanding, analyzing, and improving software and hardware systems. Assembly language is a critical tool in the reverse engineer's toolkit, enabling the dissection and reconstruction of low-level code. In the following sections of this chapter, we will explore the practical aspects of reverse engineering, including disassembly, debugging, and analysis techniques.

Section 10.2: Disassemblers and Decompilers

In the world of reverse engineering, disassemblers and decompilers are indispensable tools that aid in the analysis and reconstruction of software and hardware systems. This section explores the roles and capabilities of these tools and their significance in the reverse engineering process.

Disassemblers

Disassemblers are tools designed to convert machine code or compiled executables into human-readable assembly language code. They play a crucial role in reverse engineering by allowing engineers to examine the inner workings of a binary without access to its original source code.

Key Features of Disassemblers:

1. **Code Analysis:** Disassemblers provide a detailed view of the program's code, including instructions, registers, memory references, and control flow.

2. **Graphical Interfaces:** Many disassemblers offer graphical interfaces that visualize code flow and data structures, making it easier to understand complex programs.

3. **Annotations:** Engineers can add comments, labels, and annotations to the disassembled code, aiding in documentation and analysis.

4. **Cross-Platform Support:** Some disassemblers support multiple processor architectures, making them versatile tools for analyzing various systems.

Popular Disassemblers:

1. **IDA Pro:** IDA Pro is one of the most renowned disassemblers, known for its versatility and extensive plugin support. It is used in both professional and hobbyist reverse engineering.

2. **Ghidra:** Ghidra is an open-source disassembler developed by the National Security Agency (NSA). It offers a wide range of features and supports multiple platforms.

3. **Radare2:** Radare2 is a highly customizable and scriptable disassembler that is preferred by some reverse engineers for its flexibility.

Decompilers

Decompilers are tools that attempt to reverse the compilation process, converting low-level assembly code back into a higher-level programming language, such as C or C++. While decompilers can be immensely helpful, they face significant challenges due to the loss of information during compilation.

Key Features of Decompilers:

1. **Higher Abstraction:** Decompilers provide a more abstract view of the code, making it easier to understand for programmers who are not well-versed in assembly language.

2. **Reconstruction:** They help in reconstructing the original source code's structure, including functions, loops, and data structures.

3. **Variable Naming:** Some decompilers make educated guesses about variable and function names, improving code readability.

4. **Code Optimization:** Decompilers may attempt to optimize the decompiled code to make it more concise and efficient.

Popular Decompilers:

1. **Hex-Rays IDA Pro with Hex-Rays Decompiler:** IDA Pro offers a plugin known as Hex-Rays Decompiler, which is widely used for its ability to decompile code into C-like pseudocode.

2. **Ghidra:** Ghidra also includes a decompiler module that can translate assembly code into a C-like representation.

3. **RetDec:** RetDec is an open-source decompiler that supports various architectures and provides a useful online service for quick decompilation.

Choosing the Right Tool

The choice between a disassembler and a decompiler depends on the specific goals of the reverse engineering project. Disassemblers are essential for understanding the low-level details of a binary, while decompilers help in recovering high-level logic and structure. Many reverse engineers use both types of tools in tandem to gain a comprehensive understanding of a system.

Challenges in Decompilation

It's important to note that decompilation is not a perfect process. Challenges include:

- **Loss of Information:** Decompilers cannot recover all the information present in the original source code, leading to some loss of fidelity.

- **Ambiguity:** In cases where the original code was complex or used non-standard compiler optimizations, decompiled code may be less readable and more ambiguous.

- **Manual Verification:** The output of a decompiler often requires manual verification and correction, which can be time-consuming.

Conclusion

Disassemblers and decompilers are powerful tools in the reverse engineer's arsenal, allowing for in-depth analysis and reconstruction of software and hardware systems. While they come with their own challenges and limitations, their ability to reveal the inner workings of binaries is invaluable in various domains, including security research, software maintenance, and interoperability development. In the next sections, we will delve into practical aspects of using these tools and explore reverse engineering techniques.

Section 10.3: Analyzing Malware and Viruses

Analyzing malware and viruses is a critical aspect of computer security and threat intelligence. This section delves into the methods, tools, and practices employed by cybersecurity experts and reverse engineers to dissect and understand malicious software.

Purpose of Malware Analysis

Malware analysis serves several key purposes:

1. **Detection and Identification:** It helps in identifying and classifying malware to develop effective detection and prevention mechanisms.

2. **Behavior Analysis:** Analyzing malware allows experts to understand its behavior, including how it infects systems, communicates with command and control servers, and performs malicious actions.

3. **Reverse Engineering:** Malware analysis involves reverse engineering techniques to uncover the inner workings of the malware, such as its code structure and functionality.

4. **Attribution:** In some cases, malware analysis can provide insights into the origins and motivations of attackers, aiding in attribution.

Types of Malware Analysis

There are various approaches to malware analysis, each serving a specific purpose:

1. **Static Analysis:** Static analysis involves examining the malware without executing it. Analysts inspect the binary code, file structure, and metadata to gather information about its functionality. Tools like disassemblers and hex editors are often used for static analysis.

2. **Dynamic Analysis:** Dynamic analysis involves running the malware in a controlled environment, such as a sandbox, and monitoring its behavior. This approach reveals the malware's actions, including network communication, file modifications, and system calls.

3. **Behavioral Analysis:** Behavioral analysis focuses on observing the malware's behavior when executed. Analysts note system changes, registry modifications, and any malicious activities performed by the malware.

4. **Code Analysis:** Code analysis involves reverse engineering the malware's code to understand its functionality, algorithms, and encryption techniques. Decompilers and debuggers are commonly used in code analysis.

Malware Analysis Tools

Numerous tools are available for conducting malware analysis. Some popular ones include:

- **IDA Pro:** IDA Pro, with its disassembler and debugging capabilities, is a versatile tool for analyzing malware at the binary level.

- **Wireshark:** Wireshark is a network protocol analyzer that helps in monitoring and capturing network traffic generated by malware.

- **Cuckoo Sandbox:** Cuckoo is an open-source malware analysis platform that provides dynamic analysis in a controlled environment.

- **OllyDbg and x64dbg:** These debuggers are used for code analysis and dynamic analysis of malware.

- **YARA:** YARA is a powerful tool for creating and matching patterns in malware samples, aiding in identification and classification.

Challenges in Malware Analysis

Malware authors continually evolve their techniques to evade analysis and detection. This poses several challenges to malware analysts:

- **Obfuscation:** Malware often employs code obfuscation techniques to make analysis more difficult, such as encrypting or compressing their code.

- **Anti-Debugging:** Malware may include anti-debugging techniques to hinder efforts to analyze it using debuggers.

- **Polymorphism:** Some malware variants change their code with each infection, making it harder to identify them based on static signatures.

- **Sandbox Detection:** Malware may detect when it is running in a sandbox or virtual environment and alter its behavior to avoid detection.

Conclusion

Malware analysis is an essential practice in the field of cybersecurity. It helps in understanding and mitigating threats posed by malicious software. To effectively combat evolving malware, analysts need a combination of skills, tools, and techniques, as well as continuous learning to keep up with the latest trends in malware development and evasion. In the subsequent sections, we will explore more aspects of reverse engineering and security research, including vulnerability analysis and ethical hacking.

Section 10.4: Security Vulnerability Analysis

Security vulnerability analysis is a critical component of cybersecurity, focusing on identifying and mitigating vulnerabilities within software, systems, or networks. In this section, we will explore the processes, methodologies, and tools employed in security vulnerability analysis.

Purpose of Vulnerability Analysis

The primary purpose of vulnerability analysis is to discover and assess weaknesses or vulnerabilities that could be exploited by attackers. By identifying and addressing these vulnerabilities, organizations can enhance their security posture and protect their assets and data.

Vulnerability Assessment vs. Penetration Testing

Vulnerability analysis often involves two key activities: vulnerability assessment and penetration testing.

1. **Vulnerability Assessment:** A vulnerability assessment is a systematic review of an organization's systems and networks to identify known vulnerabilities. It typically relies on automated tools and databases of known vulnerabilities. The output is a list of vulnerabilities that need to be addressed.

2. **Penetration Testing:** Penetration testing, or ethical hacking, goes a step further. It involves actively attempting to exploit vulnerabilities to determine their real-world impact. Penetration testers simulate attacks to assess the organization's security posture comprehensively.

Methodologies for Vulnerability Analysis

Several methodologies guide vulnerability analysis processes:

1. **Common Vulnerability Scoring System (CVSS):** CVSS provides a standardized method for assessing the severity of vulnerabilities. It considers factors such as exploitability, impact, and access complexity to assign a score.

2. **OWASP Top Ten:** The Open Web Application Security Project (OWASP) maintains a list of the top ten web application vulnerabilities. This list helps organizations prioritize their efforts to secure web applications.

3. **MITRE ATT&CK Framework:** The MITRE ATT&CK (Adversarial Tactics, Techniques, and Common Knowledge) framework provides a comprehensive matrix of adversary behaviors and tactics. It assists in understanding and mitigating threats effectively.

Vulnerability Analysis Tools

A range of tools is available for vulnerability analysis, including:

- **Nessus:** Nessus is a widely used vulnerability scanner that identifies known vulnerabilities in systems and networks.

- **Burp Suite:** Burp Suite is a web vulnerability scanner and proxy tool for web application security testing.

- **Metasploit:** Metasploit is a powerful framework for penetration testing and developing exploit code.

- **Wireshark:** Wireshark is a network protocol analyzer that helps in monitoring and analyzing network traffic for potential vulnerabilities.

Challenges in Vulnerability Analysis

Vulnerability analysis faces several challenges:

- **Zero-Day Vulnerabilities:** These are vulnerabilities for which no patches or fixes are available. Identifying and mitigating zero-day vulnerabilities is exceptionally challenging.

- **Complexity:** Modern software and systems are complex, making it difficult to identify all potential vulnerabilities comprehensively.

- **False Positives:** Vulnerability scanners may produce false positives, requiring manual verification.

- **Patch Management:** Applying patches to fix vulnerabilities can be challenging in large organizations with complex IT environments.

Conclusion

Security vulnerability analysis is a critical aspect of cybersecurity, helping organizations proactively identify and mitigate security weaknesses. By using methodologies, tools, and best practices, security professionals can stay ahead of potential threats and minimize the risk of exploitation. In the subsequent sections, we will explore ethical hacking and the use of assembly language in security-related tasks.

Section 10.5: Ethical Hacking with Assembly

Ethical hacking, often referred to as "white-hat hacking," involves intentionally probing and testing computer systems, networks, and software applications to identify security vulnerabilities. Ethical hackers use the same techniques as malicious hackers but do so with the permission of the system owner to improve security. In this section, we'll explore the role of assembly language in ethical hacking and its applications.

Assembly language is a powerful tool in the toolkit of ethical hackers. Here are some ways it plays a crucial role:

1. **Exploit Development:** Ethical hackers use assembly language to develop exploits for vulnerabilities they discover. Writing low-level code in assembly allows them to craft precise and efficient exploits.

2. **Reverse Engineering:** Assembly language is essential for reverse engineering binary executables and firmware. Ethical hackers disassemble and analyze software to understand its behavior and identify vulnerabilities.

3. **Shellcode:** In many hacking scenarios, attackers need to inject custom code into a target system, often referred to as shellcode. This code is typically written in assembly language to ensure it's compact and runs without dependencies.

4. **Kernel-Level Exploits:** Some vulnerabilities exist at the kernel level of an operating system. To exploit these, hackers often write assembly code that interacts directly with the kernel.

Assembly Language-Based Attacks

Ethical hackers use assembly language for various types of attacks, including:

- **Buffer Overflow Exploits:** Writing assembly code to exploit buffer overflows is a common practice. By overwriting memory, attackers can gain control over a vulnerable system.

- **ROP (Return-Oriented Programming):** Assembly language is used to construct ROP chains, a technique for redirecting the flow of a program without introducing new code. This is useful in bypassing security mechanisms.

- **Shellcode Execution:** When attackers gain control of a program's execution flow, they often inject shellcode written in assembly language to provide a backdoor or establish control.

Tools and Frameworks

Ethical hackers leverage several tools and frameworks that include assembly language:

- **Metasploit:** Metasploit, a widely used penetration testing framework, allows users to develop, test, and execute exploits, many of which are written in assembly.

- **IDA Pro:** IDA Pro is a popular disassembler and debugger used for reverse engineering. It provides assembly code analysis and visualization capabilities.

- **Assembly Language IDEs:** Some ethical hackers prefer using integrated development environments (IDEs) tailored for assembly, such as Radare2 or Hopper.

Ethical hacking must adhere to strict legal and ethical guidelines. Hackers must have proper authorization to test systems and networks. Unauthorized hacking is illegal and can lead to severe consequences.

Additionally, ethical hackers must ensure they use their skills responsibly and for the benefit of organizations or society as a whole. They play a vital role in improving security and protecting against malicious cyber threats.

Conclusion

Assembly language is a valuable skill for ethical hackers who aim to uncover and address security vulnerabilities. It empowers them to write precise and efficient code for exploitation and reverse engineering. When used responsibly and ethically, assembly language contributes to the overall security of computer systems and networks. In the following chapters, we will delve into other applications of assembly language, including game development, performance optimization, and more.

Chapter 11: Assembly Language for Game Development 11.1 Game Development Basics

In this section, we will delve into the fundamental concepts of game development with assembly language. Game development is a field where performance and control over hardware are crucial, making assembly language an excellent choice for creating games that push the limits of what is possible on a given platform.

Game Development Basics

Game development is the process of creating interactive digital experiences that entertain, engage, and challenge players. These experiences, known as video games, can range from simple 2D platformers to complex 3D worlds, and they often involve a combination of art, sound, story, and gameplay.

The Role of Assembly Language in Game Development

Assembly language plays a unique role in game development, offering several advantages:

1. **Performance:** Games demand high performance to render graphics, simulate physics, and respond to player input in real-time. Assembly allows developers to write code that is finely tuned to the hardware, maximizing performance.

2. **Low-Level Control:** Game developers often need to control hardware resources like graphics cards and input devices directly. Assembly provides the necessary low-level control to interact with these devices efficiently.

3. **Portability:** Assembly code can be highly portable, especially when targeting specific hardware platforms. This is essential for console and embedded game development.

4. **Optimization:** Assembly is ideal for optimizing critical sections of game code, such as rendering and physics calculations, to ensure smooth gameplay.

Graphics Programming in Assembly

One of the core aspects of game development is graphics programming. In this subsection, we will briefly explore how assembly language is used for graphics rendering:

- **Pixel Manipulation:** Assembly allows developers to manipulate individual pixels, making it suitable for tasks like creating visual effects or procedural content generation.

- **Vector Operations:** Modern games often use vector operations for transformations, lighting, and collision detection. Assembly provides efficient support for vector mathematics.

- **GPU Programming:** Some game engines use assembly-like languages to program the GPU directly. These "shader" languages enable advanced rendering techniques.

Game Physics and Collision Detection

Physics simulation is another critical component of many games, especially those involving realistic motion and interaction. Assembly language can be used for:

- **Physics Calculations:** Assembly's speed and precision make it well-suited for physics calculations, including rigid body dynamics and particle systems.

- **Collision Detection:** Accurate collision detection algorithms can be implemented in assembly to handle complex interactions between game objects.

Audio and Input Handling

Game development also involves audio and input processing. Assembly's low-level capabilities are beneficial for:

- **Real-Time Audio:** Assembly can be used to process and generate audio in real-time, enabling advanced sound effects and music.

- **Input Handling:** Low-level input handling ensures responsiveness to player actions, making assembly a valuable tool for managing user input.

Creating a Simple Game in Assembly

To illustrate the concepts discussed in this section, we will provide an example of creating a simple game in assembly language. This example will cover basic graphics rendering, player input, and game logic, demonstrating how assembly can be used to develop engaging interactive experiences.

In the following chapters, we will dive deeper into various aspects of game development with assembly, exploring advanced graphics techniques, game engines, and case studies of real-world game projects.

Chapter 11: Assembly Language for Game Development

Section 11.1: Game Development Basics

In this section, we will delve into the fundamental concepts of game development with assembly language. Game development is a field where performance and control over hardware are crucial, making assembly language an excellent choice for creating games that push the limits of what is possible on a given platform.

Game Development Basics

Game development is the process of creating interactive digital experiences that entertain, engage, and challenge players. These experiences, known as video games, can range from simple 2D platformers to complex 3D worlds, and they often involve a combination of art, sound, story, and gameplay.

The Role of Assembly Language in Game Development

Assembly language plays a unique role in game development, offering several advantages:

1. **Performance:** Games demand high performance to render graphics, simulate physics, and respond to player input in real-time. Assembly allows developers to write code that is finely tuned to the hardware, maximizing performance.

2. **Low-Level Control:** Game developers often need to control hardware resources like graphics cards and input devices directly. Assembly provides the necessary low-level control to interact with these devices efficiently.

3. **Portability:** Assembly code can be highly portable, especially when targeting specific hardware platforms. This is essential for console and embedded game development.

4. **Optimization:** Assembly is ideal for optimizing critical sections of game code, such as rendering and physics calculations, to ensure smooth gameplay.

Graphics Programming in Assembly

One of the core aspects of game development is graphics programming. In this subsection, we will briefly explore how assembly language is used for graphics rendering:

- **Pixel Manipulation:** Assembly allows developers to manipulate individual pixels, making it suitable for tasks like creating visual effects or procedural content generation.

- **Vector Operations:** Modern games often use vector operations for transformations, lighting, and collision detection. Assembly provides efficient support for vector mathematics.

- **GPU Programming:** Some game engines use assembly-like languages to program the GPU directly. These "shader" languages enable advanced rendering techniques.

Physics simulation is another critical component of many games, especially those involving realistic motion and interaction. Assembly language can be used for:

- **Physics Calculations:** Assembly's speed and precision make it well-suited for physics calculations, including rigid body dynamics and particle systems.

- **Collision Detection:** Accurate collision detection algorithms can be implemented in assembly to handle complex interactions between game objects.

Audio and Input Handling

Game development also involves audio and input processing. Assembly's low-level capabilities are beneficial for:

- **Real-Time Audio:** Assembly can be used to process and generate audio in real-time, enabling advanced sound effects and music.

- **Input Handling:** Low-level input handling ensures responsiveness to player actions, making assembly a valuable tool for managing user input.

Creating a Simple Game in Assembly

To illustrate the concepts discussed in this section, we will provide an example of creating a simple game in assembly language. This example will cover basic graphics rendering, player input, and game logic, demonstrating how assembly can be used to develop engaging interactive experiences.

In the following chapters, we will dive deeper into various aspects of game development with assembly, exploring advanced graphics techniques, game engines, and case studies of real-world game projects.

Section 11.2: Graphics Programming in Assembly

In the realm of game development, graphics programming holds a pivotal role. It involves rendering 2D and 3D graphics, handling shaders, and managing the visual aspects of games. In this section, we will explore how assembly language can be used for graphics programming and its significance in creating visually appealing games.

The Importance of Graphics Programming

Graphics programming in games encompasses a wide range of tasks, including rendering characters, environments, special effects, and animations. The visual quality of a game directly impacts the player's experience and immersion, making it a critical aspect of game development.

Assembly and Graphics Programming

Assembly language is well-suited for graphics programming due to the following advantages:

1. **Low-Level Control:** Assembly provides developers with precise control over hardware resources, making it ideal for interacting with graphics hardware like GPUs (Graphics Processing Units).

2. **Efficiency:** Graphics rendering often involves performing complex mathematical operations on large datasets. Assembly's efficiency and optimization capabilities enable developers to achieve real-time rendering, even in demanding scenarios.

3. **Vector Operations:** Many graphics operations involve vector mathematics, such as transformations, rotations, and scaling. Assembly excels in handling vector operations efficiently.

Rendering Techniques in Assembly

Graphics rendering in assembly language involves several fundamental techniques:

1. Pixel Manipulation:

Assembly allows developers to manipulate individual pixels in the framebuffer. This level of control is essential for tasks like creating visual effects, generating procedural content, or implementing pixel-based art styles.

2. Vector Graphics:

Assembly can efficiently handle vector graphics by performing mathematical operations on vectors. This capability is crucial for rendering 2D shapes and scenes.

3. 3D Rendering:

For 3D graphics, assembly language is used to perform transformations, lighting calculations, and perspective projections. Developers can create 3D scenes with realistic lighting and shading effects.

4. Shaders:

Shaders are small programs that run on the GPU to control various aspects of rendering, such as vertex and fragment shading. Assembly-like languages are often used to write shaders, offering fine-grained control over the rendering pipeline.

Example: Pixel Manipulation in Assembly

```
; Example code in x86 assembly for pixel manipulation
; This code sets a pixel at (x, y) in a framebuffer to a specified color.
```

```asm
section .data
    framebuffer db 320*200   ; Assuming a 320x200 pixel framebuffer
    x db 100                 ; X-coordinate of the pixel
    y db 50                  ; Y-coordinate of the pixel
    color db 255             ; Color (0-255)

section .text
global main
main:
    ; Calculate the pixel offset in the framebuffer
    mov al, [y]
    imul ax, 320             ; Multiply y by the width (320 pixels)
    add ax, [x]              ; Add x to the offset
    mov di, ax               ; Store the offset in di (destination index)

    ; Set the pixel color
    mov al, [color]
    mov [framebuffer + di], al

    ; Exit
    mov ah, 0x4c             ; DOS function 4C (terminate program)
    int 0x21
```

This example demonstrates a simple pixel manipulation routine in x86 assembly, setting the color of a pixel at a specified position in a hypothetical framebuffer.

In upcoming sections, we will explore advanced graphics techniques, including 3D rendering, shaders, and integrating assembly with game engines to create visually stunning games.

Section 11.3: Game Physics and Collision Detection

In the realm of game development, creating realistic and engaging game physics is crucial for delivering an immersive player experience. Game physics govern how objects interact with each other and the virtual world, determining movements, collisions, and reactions. In this section, we will delve into the significance of game physics and the role of assembly language in implementing these physics systems.

The Importance of Game Physics

Game physics simulate the physical laws of the real world within the game environment. They add authenticity and challenge to gameplay, making interactions feel believable. Key aspects of game physics include:

- **Object Movement:** Physics calculations control how objects move, considering factors like gravity, acceleration, and friction.

- **Collision Detection:** Detecting collisions between objects is vital for ensuring that characters and objects interact realistically.

- **Rigid Body Dynamics:** Simulation of rigid body physics allows for complex interactions between objects, such as stacking, rolling, and bouncing.

- **Particle Systems:** Simulating particle systems enables effects like fire, smoke, and explosions, contributing to the overall visual appeal of games.

Assembly and Game Physics

Assembly language can play a significant role in implementing game physics due to its low-level control and optimization capabilities. Here's why assembly is relevant:

1. **Performance:** Real-time physics simulations demand high performance. Assembly's efficiency and fine-grained control can optimize calculations for smoother gameplay.

2. **Low-Level Access:** Assembly provides direct access to hardware resources, making it suitable for tasks like collision detection and response.

3. **Customization:** Developers can fine-tune physics algorithms to match the specific requirements of their games, achieving unique and engaging gameplay.

Collision Detection in Assembly

Collision detection is a fundamental component of game physics. It involves identifying when two objects intersect in the game world. Here's a simplified example of collision detection in assembly-like pseudocode:

```
; Example pseudocode for basic collision detection
; Detect collision between two rectangles

; Define the properties of Rectangle A
RectA_X = 100
RectA_Y = 100
RectA_Width = 50
RectA_Height = 50

; Define the properties of Rectangle B
RectB_X = 120
RectB_Y = 120
RectB_Width = 60
RectB_Height = 60

; Check for collision
if (RectA_X < RectB_X + RectB_Width &&
    RectA_X + RectA_Width > RectB_X &&
    RectA_Y < RectB_Y + RectB_Height &&
    RectA_Y + RectA_Height > RectB_Y) {
```

```
    ; Collision detected, perform appropriate actions
    HandleCollision()
}
```

In this example, we check for a collision between two rectangles using simple bounding box collision detection. If a collision is detected, the `HandleCollision()` function is called to handle the interaction between the objects.

Advanced game engines often use more sophisticated algorithms, such as separating axis theorem (SAT) or swept AABB (axis-aligned bounding box) collision detection, to achieve accurate and efficient collision detection in assembly or assembly-like languages.

In upcoming sections, we will explore further aspects of game development in assembly, including audio and input handling, as well as creating a simple game using assembly language.

Section 11.4: Audio and Input Handling

In the world of game development, audio and input handling are critical components that contribute to the overall player experience. This section will explore the importance of audio and input in games and how assembly language can be utilized to manage these aspects effectively.

The Role of Audio in Games

Audio enriches games by providing immersive soundscapes, music, and interactive audio cues. It plays a pivotal role in conveying information, creating ambiance, and enhancing emotional engagement. Key aspects of audio in games include:

- **Sound Effects:** These include footsteps, weapon fire, and environmental sounds that provide auditory feedback to player actions.

- **Background Music:** Music sets the mood and atmosphere of the game, intensifying emotions and tension.

- **Voiceovers:** Dialogues and voice acting bring characters and narratives to life.

- **Interactive Audio:** Sound may react dynamically to in-game events, enhancing realism.

Assembly Language for Audio

Assembly language can be used to optimize audio processing in games. Real-time audio synthesis and manipulation benefit from assembly's low-level control and efficiency. Here are ways assembly can be involved:

1. **Digital Signal Processing (DSP):** Assembly is well-suited for DSP tasks like filtering, modulation, and effects processing.

2. **Low-Latency Audio:** Games require low audio latency to maintain synchronization with gameplay. Assembly can reduce processing time, ensuring minimal delay.

3. **Custom Audio Engines:** Developers can create custom audio engines tailored to their games, allowing for unique audio experiences.

Input Handling in Assembly

Accurate and responsive input handling is crucial for delivering a satisfying gaming experience. Player input can come from various sources, including keyboards, mice, gamepads, and touchscreens. Assembly language can be used for efficient input processing due to its low-level capabilities. Here's how assembly contributes to input handling:

1. **Polling Input Devices:** Assembly code can directly interface with input devices, polling them for input state changes.

2. **Custom Input Mappings:** Developers can create custom input mappings and processing logic to interpret player actions accurately.

3. **Reducing Input Lag:** Assembly's speed and efficiency ensure minimal input lag, enhancing player responsiveness.

Sample Input Handling in Assembly-Like Pseudocode

Below is a simplified example of keyboard input handling in assembly-like pseudocode:

```
; Example pseudocode for keyboard input handling
; Detect if the 'Space' key is pressed

; Define key codes
KEY_SPACE = 32

; Poll keyboard input
PollKeyboardInput()

; Check if 'Space' key is pressed
if (IsKeyPressed(KEY_SPACE)) {
    ; Perform action when 'Space' is pressed
    Jump()
}
```

In this example, we define a key code for the 'Space' key and periodically poll the keyboard for input. If the 'Space' key is detected as pressed, we trigger the Jump() action in response.

Advanced game engines and frameworks offer more sophisticated input handling, including support for multiple input devices, customizable key bindings, and event-driven input systems. Assembly language can be integrated into these engines to optimize performance-critical input processing routines.

In the following section, we will explore the complexities of game physics and collision detection, further advancing our understanding of game development in assembly.

Section 11.5: Creating a Simple Game in Assembly

In this section, we will delve into the process of creating a simple game using assembly language. Game development in assembly can be challenging but rewarding, offering fine-grained control over every aspect of the game's behavior. We will outline the basic steps involved in developing a text-based game as an illustrative example.

Game Design and Concept

Before diving into code, it's crucial to have a clear game design and concept. For our simple game, let's create a text-based "Guess the Number" game. The player's objective will be to guess a random number within a specified range.

Pseudocode for the Game

Let's outline the game's logic in pseudocode before implementing it in assembly:

```
1. Generate a random number within a specified range (e.g., 1-100).
2. Display a welcome message and game instructions.
3. Initialize a variable to store the player's guess count.
4. Loop until the player guesses the correct number:
   a. Prompt the player to enter a guess.
   b. Read and validate the player's input.
   c. Compare the guess with the random number:
      - If the guess is correct, congratulate the player and display the numb
er of attempts.
      - If the guess is too high or too low, provide feedback.
   d. Increment the guess count.
5. Ask if the player wants to play again.
6. If yes, generate a new random number and repeat the game.
7. If no, display a farewell message and end the game.
```

Assembly Implementation

Creating a game in assembly requires a deep understanding of low-level programming concepts. You'll need to work with input/output, random number generation, loops, conditionals, and more. The code can be quite extensive, so we'll provide an overview of key assembly code sections:

1. **Initializing Variables:** In assembly, you'll need to allocate memory to store variables like the random number, player's guess, and guess count.

2. **Random Number Generation:** You can use assembly's ability to work with hardware and time to generate pseudo-random numbers.

3. **Input/Output Handling:** Implement input prompts, reading player input, and displaying messages. These often involve system calls or interrupts.

4. **Looping and Conditionals:** Use assembly's branching instructions for game loops and conditionals, allowing the game to respond to player input.

5. **Game Logic:** Implement the core game logic following the pseudocode, including comparing guesses and checking for victory conditions.

6. **Memory Management:** Efficiently manage memory to avoid issues like memory leaks.

7. **Error Handling:** Implement error handling and input validation to ensure the game behaves predictably.

Developing a game in assembly is a complex task, and the provided pseudocode is just a simplified representation. In practice, you'd need to work with a specific assembly language and development environment, potentially making use of libraries or system functions for certain tasks.

While text-based games like "Guess the Number" are a good starting point, more complex games with graphical elements would require even more intricate assembly code. Nonetheless, creating games in assembly can be a rewarding way to gain a deeper understanding of computer systems and programming.

Chapter 12: Assembly Language for Performance Optimization

Section 12.1: Profiling and Benchmarking

Profiling and benchmarking are essential practices in assembly language programming to optimize the performance of your code. In this section, we will explore the concepts of profiling and benchmarking, how they can help identify bottlenecks in your assembly programs, and strategies for improving performance.

Profiling

Profiling involves analyzing the execution of a program to identify which parts of the code consume the most time and resources. This information helps you focus your optimization efforts on the critical sections. Profiling can be done using various tools and techniques, including:

- **Instruction-Level Profiling:** This involves tracking the number of times each instruction is executed. Tools like perf on Linux or profilers specific to your assembly development environment can provide this information.

- **Function-Level Profiling:** Profilers can also identify which functions or subroutines consume the most time. This helps in pinpointing areas that need optimization.

- **Memory Profiling:** Profiling tools can reveal memory usage patterns, such as excessive memory allocation or deallocation, which can impact performance.

Profiling is an iterative process. After identifying performance bottlenecks, you can make optimizations, reprofile, and verify the improvements.

Benchmarking

Benchmarking involves measuring the execution time of a piece of code to compare different implementations or optimizations. It's essential to have well-defined benchmarks to assess the impact of changes accurately. Some considerations for benchmarking in assembly programming include:

- **Stability:** Ensure that your benchmarking environment is stable and not affected by external factors.

- **Repeatable:** Benchmarks should be repeatable, producing consistent results on each run.

- **Isolation:** Benchmark only the specific code or algorithm you want to test, isolating it from unrelated parts of your program.

- **Baseline:** Create a baseline benchmark to compare against when making optimizations. This helps quantify the improvements achieved.

Once you've profiled your code and identified performance bottlenecks, you can apply various optimization strategies in assembly programming:

- **Algorithmic Optimizations:** Consider improving the algorithm or data structures used in your code to reduce computational complexity.

- **Loop Unrolling:** Manually unroll loops to reduce loop overhead and take advantage of instruction-level parallelism.

- **SIMD Instructions:** Use Single Instruction, Multiple Data (SIMD) instructions to perform parallel processing of data.

- **Reducing Memory Access:** Minimize memory access, especially costly cache misses, by optimizing data access patterns.

- **Instruction Selection:** Choose instructions that are more efficient in terms of execution time and resource usage.

- **Compiler Optimizations:** If you are working with a high-level language that compiles to assembly, explore compiler optimization flags and techniques.

Case Study

As a case study in this section, we'll take a closer look at profiling and optimizing a real-world assembly program. We'll demonstrate how to identify bottlenecks, make optimizations, and measure the impact on performance. This hands-on example will provide valuable insights into the optimization process in assembly language programming.

Optimizing assembly code is a complex but rewarding task that can lead to substantial performance improvements. Profiling and benchmarking are indispensable tools in your optimization toolkit, helping you identify areas for improvement and measure the effectiveness of your optimizations. In the subsequent sections of this chapter, we will explore more advanced optimization techniques and real-world case studies to deepen your understanding of assembly language performance optimization.

Section 12.2: Optimization Techniques

In the previous section, we discussed the importance of profiling and benchmarking in optimizing assembly code. In this section, we'll delve deeper into various optimization techniques commonly used in assembly language programming. These techniques are essential for achieving maximum performance from your code.

1. Algorithmic Optimization

Optimizing the algorithm or data structure used in your code can often yield the most significant performance improvements. This involves selecting or designing algorithms that are more efficient in terms of time and space complexity. For example, switching from a brute-force search algorithm to a more sophisticated search algorithm like binary search can greatly reduce execution time.

2. Loop Unrolling

Loop unrolling is a manual optimization technique that aims to reduce loop overhead and take advantage of instruction-level parallelism. Instead of executing a loop with a fixed number of iterations, you manually write out multiple copies of the loop body. This allows the compiler and processor to better optimize the code by interleaving instructions from different iterations.

Here's a simple example in x86 assembly that demonstrates loop unrolling:

```
; Original loop with 4 iterations
mov ecx, 4
loop_start:
    ; Loop body here
    ; ...

    dec ecx
    jnz loop_start

; Unrolled loop with 4 iterations
; Iteration 1
    ; Loop body for iteration 1
    ; ...
; Iteration 2
    ; Loop body for iteration 2
    ; ...
; Iteration 3
    ; Loop body for iteration 3
    ; ...
; Iteration 4
    ; Loop body for iteration 4
    ; ...
```

3. SIMD (Single Instruction, Multiple Data) Instructions

SIMD instructions allow you to perform parallel processing of data. These instructions operate on multiple data elements simultaneously, which can significantly speed up certain operations like vectorized mathematical calculations. Popular SIMD instruction sets include Intel's SSE and AVX extensions and ARM NEON.

For example, here's a simple SIMD code snippet that adds two vectors of floating-point numbers in x86 assembly using SSE:

```
; Assuming xmm0 and xmm1 contain two vectors of floats
addps xmm0, xmm1   ; Add xmm0 and xmm1 element-wise
```

4. Minimizing Memory Access

Memory access is often a performance bottleneck, especially when dealing with large datasets. Optimizing data access patterns to reduce costly cache misses is crucial. Techniques like data prefetching, using smaller data types, and reordering data structures for better locality can help minimize memory access times.

5. Instruction Selection

Choosing the right instructions for your code can make a significant difference in execution time and resource usage. Modern processors have complex pipelines and execution units, and selecting instructions that match the processor's capabilities can lead to more efficient code.

6. Compiler Optimizations

If you are writing high-level code that compiles to assembly, explore compiler optimization flags and techniques. Compilers can perform a wide range of optimizations, including constant folding, function inlining, and instruction scheduling, to generate efficient assembly code.

7. Profiling and Benchmarking (Revisited)

Remember that profiling and benchmarking should be an integral part of the optimization process. After applying optimization techniques, profile your code again to ensure that the changes have had the desired impact on performance. Benchmarking helps quantify the improvements achieved by the optimizations.

In the next section, we will dive into more advanced optimization strategies and explore real-world case studies where these techniques are applied to assembly code. These examples will provide practical insights into optimizing assembly language programs for various scenarios.

Section 12.3: Vectorization and SIMD Instructions

Vectorization is a powerful optimization technique used in assembly language programming to exploit the parallel processing capabilities of modern CPUs. This technique involves performing multiple identical operations on data elements simultaneously using Single Instruction, Multiple Data (SIMD) instructions. SIMD instructions are available on most modern CPUs and allow you to process data in parallel, greatly improving performance for tasks that involve large datasets or repetitive calculations.

Understanding SIMD

SIMD instructions operate on multiple data elements in a single instruction, making them highly efficient for tasks like image processing, audio processing, and scientific computing. SIMD registers, such as the XMM registers in x86 architecture, can hold multiple data elements, like floats or integers, packed into a single register.

For example, consider the task of adding two arrays of floating-point numbers element-wise. In traditional scalar code, you would use a loop to iterate through the arrays and add each pair of elements one by one. However, with SIMD instructions, you can add multiple pairs of elements in a single instruction, significantly reducing the number of instructions executed.

Here's a simplified example in x86 assembly using SSE (Streaming SIMD Extensions):

```
; Assuming xmm0 and xmm1 contain two arrays of floats
addps xmm0, xmm1   ; Add the arrays element-wise
```

In this code, the addps instruction adds four pairs of floats from xmm0 and xmm1 simultaneously.

Benefits of Vectorization

Vectorization offers several benefits, including:

1. **Improved Performance:** By processing multiple data elements in parallel, SIMD instructions can significantly speed up computations, making them ideal for tasks that involve large datasets or repetitive calculations.

2. **Reduced Instruction Overhead:** Since SIMD instructions perform multiple operations in one instruction, there is less overhead associated with instruction fetching and decoding.

3. **Simplified Code:** Vectorized code can often be more concise and easier to read than equivalent scalar code with explicit loops.

Considerations and Challenges

While vectorization can provide substantial performance gains, it's essential to be aware of some considerations and challenges:

1. **Data Alignment:** SIMD instructions often require data to be aligned in memory correctly. Misaligned data can result in performance penalties or even crashes.

2. **Data Dependencies:** Some operations may have dependencies between data elements, making them unsuitable for vectorization. It's essential to identify and handle such cases.

3. **Compiler Support:** Compilers can automatically vectorize code, but manual vectorization may be necessary for fine-grained control. Understanding your compiler's capabilities is essential.

4. **Portability:** SIMD instruction sets vary between CPU architectures (e.g., SSE for x86, NEON for ARM). Writing portable code may require handling multiple instruction sets or using libraries that abstract these differences.

In practice, vectorization is a valuable tool for optimizing performance-critical sections of code, especially in domains like multimedia processing, scientific computing, and simulations. However, it requires a good understanding of both the problem domain and the specific SIMD instruction set being used. When used judiciously, vectorization can result in substantial performance improvements in assembly language programs.

Section 12.4: Multithreading and Parallelism

Multithreading and parallelism are essential concepts in modern assembly language programming for achieving high-performance computing. They enable a program to execute multiple threads or tasks concurrently, taking full advantage of multi-core processors. In this section, we will explore how assembly language can be used to implement multithreading and parallelism, along with their benefits and challenges.

Understanding Multithreading

Multithreading involves breaking a program into multiple threads, each of which can execute independently and concurrently. These threads share the same memory space, allowing them to communicate and synchronize their operations efficiently. Multithreading is particularly valuable for tasks that can be divided into smaller, independent subtasks that can be executed simultaneously.

In assembly language, multithreading can be implemented using thread libraries and system-specific instructions for thread management. For example, on x86 architecture, the Windows API provides functions for creating and managing threads.

Benefits of Multithreading

Multithreading offers several advantages, including:

1. **Improved Performance:** Multithreaded programs can execute multiple tasks in parallel, making effective use of multi-core processors and significantly improving performance for tasks that can be parallelized.

2. **Responsiveness:** Multithreading allows a program to remain responsive even when performing computationally intensive tasks. For example, a graphical user interface (GUI) can continue to handle user input while a background thread performs calculations.

3. **Resource Utilization:** Multithreading can better utilize available system resources, reducing idle time and maximizing CPU usage.

While multithreading can deliver substantial performance improvements, it also presents challenges and considerations:

1. **Concurrency Control:** Threads may access shared data simultaneously, leading to race conditions and data corruption. Proper synchronization mechanisms, such as locks and semaphores, are essential to avoid these issues.

2. **Complexity:** Multithreaded code is often more complex and challenging to debug than single-threaded code. Deadlocks, thread contention, and other concurrency-related bugs can be hard to identify and fix.

3. **Portability:** Assembly language multithreading code may be platform-specific, making it less portable. It's important to consider portability when targeting multiple architectures.

4. **Scalability:** Not all tasks are suitable for multithreading. Some algorithms have limited parallelism potential, and forcing multithreading may not lead to performance gains.

Parallelism

Parallelism refers to the execution of multiple tasks simultaneously, whether on separate processors or cores (hardware parallelism) or within a single processor via instruction-level parallelism (ILP) and pipelining (software parallelism).

In assembly language, you can leverage hardware parallelism by designing your code to take advantage of multi-core processors. This may involve using processor-specific instructions or libraries that provide parallelism support.

Benefits of Parallelism

Parallelism offers several benefits, including:

1. **Efficiency:** Parallel execution can significantly reduce the time required to complete computationally intensive tasks by distributing the workload across multiple cores or processors.

2. **Scalability:** As more cores become available on modern processors, parallelism allows your programs to scale their performance accordingly.

3. **Real-Time Processing:** Parallelism is crucial for real-time applications, such as multimedia processing and scientific simulations, where timely execution of tasks is essential.

Challenges and Considerations

Parallelism introduces its own set of challenges:

1. **Load Balancing:** Ensuring that tasks are evenly distributed across cores can be challenging. Load imbalances can lead to suboptimal performance.

2. **Data Dependencies:** Dependencies between tasks can limit parallelism. Identifying and managing these dependencies is critical.

3. **Synchronization Overhead:** When tasks need to synchronize or communicate, the overhead of synchronization mechanisms (e.g., locks) can affect performance.

4. **Amdahl's Law:** Amdahl's Law states that the speedup of a program due to parallelism is limited by the fraction of the code that cannot be parallelized. Understanding this law is essential for setting realistic performance expectations.

In conclusion, multithreading and parallelism are vital techniques for achieving high performance in assembly language programming. However, they require careful consideration of synchronization, data dependencies, and platform-specific optimizations. When applied effectively, these techniques can unlock the full potential of modern processors for computationally intensive tasks.

Section 12.5: Achieving High Performance in Assembly

Achieving high performance in assembly language programming involves optimizing code to execute as efficiently as possible. In this section, we'll explore various techniques and considerations for optimizing assembly code to maximize execution speed and resource utilization.

1. Profiling and Benchmarking

Optimization begins with identifying performance bottlenecks. Profiling tools allow you to analyze your code's execution and pinpoint areas that require optimization. Profilers provide insights into which functions or code sections consume the most CPU time, memory, or other resources.

Once bottlenecks are identified, benchmarking can help assess the impact of optimizations. Benchmarking involves measuring the execution time of different code versions to determine which one performs better.

2. Optimization Techniques

Several optimization techniques can be applied in assembly language:

- **Loop Unrolling:** Expanding loops by replicating loop bodies to reduce loop overhead. This can lead to better pipelining and instruction-level parallelism.

- **Instruction Scheduling:** Reordering instructions to minimize stalls and dependencies. This can be challenging in assembly due to limited registers and complex dependencies.

- **Register Allocation:** Efficient use of registers is crucial. Avoiding unnecessary spills to memory and managing register dependencies are essential.

- **Inline Assembly:** When using a high-level language, inline assembly allows you to insert assembly code directly into your source code, optimizing specific sections for performance.

3. Vectorization and SIMD Instructions

Modern processors support Single Instruction, Multiple Data (SIMD) instructions. These instructions operate on multiple data elements simultaneously, significantly improving performance for data-parallel tasks. Understanding and utilizing SIMD instructions is vital for achieving high performance.

4. Multithreading and Parallelism

As discussed in the previous section, multithreading and parallelism can be harnessed to distribute workloads across multiple cores or processors, achieving parallel execution and improved performance.

5. Compiler Optimizations

Some assembly code is generated by compilers. Compiler optimizations can greatly impact code performance. Understanding how to write code that optimizes well under compiler analysis is valuable.

6. Cache Optimization

Memory access patterns significantly affect performance. Optimizing code for cache locality can reduce cache misses, which can be a major performance bottleneck. Techniques like loop tiling and prefetching can help.

7. Profile-Guided Optimization

Profile-guided optimization (PGO) involves using profiling data from real program runs to guide optimizations. PGO can help the compiler make informed decisions about code restructuring and inlining, resulting in better performance.

8. Minimizing Branching

Branch instructions can introduce pipeline stalls. Minimizing branches by using conditional move instructions (e.g., CMOVcc) or predicated execution can enhance performance.

9. Software Pipelining

Software pipelining is a technique where loop iterations overlap to minimize stalls and maximize throughput. This can be complex to implement but offers significant performance gains.

10. Critical Path Analysis

Identifying and optimizing the critical path of your code, the portion that takes the longest to execute, can lead to substantial performance improvements. Profiling tools can assist in identifying the critical path.

11. Documentation and Maintainability

Optimization should not compromise code readability and maintainability. Detailed comments and documentation are crucial to ensure that optimized code remains understandable to others and your future self.

In conclusion, achieving high performance in assembly language programming requires a combination of careful analysis, optimization techniques, and a deep understanding of the underlying hardware. Profiling, benchmarking, and utilizing SIMD instructions are essential tools in the optimization process. Keep in mind that optimization should always be guided by the specific requirements of your application and the trade-offs between performance and maintainability.

Chapter 13: Assembly Language for IoT Devices

Internet of Things (IoT) devices are becoming increasingly prevalent in our connected world. These embedded systems range from small sensors and microcontrollers to more powerful IoT gateways and edge devices. Assembly language programming plays a significant role in developing software for IoT devices due to its ability to provide fine-grained control over hardware resources and deliver efficient code. In this chapter, we'll explore how assembly language is utilized in the realm of IoT.

Section 13.1: IoT Device Architecture

Before delving into assembly language programming for IoT devices, it's essential to understand the architecture of these devices. IoT devices typically consist of the following components:

1. Microcontroller or Microprocessor

At the heart of an IoT device is a microcontroller or microprocessor. These chips serve as the brain of the device, executing instructions and managing data. Assembly language programming directly targets these processors, allowing for precise control over their functionality.

2. Sensors and Actuators

IoT devices interact with the physical world through sensors (e.g., temperature sensors, motion detectors) and actuators (e.g., motors, relays). Assembly code is used to read data from sensors and control actuators efficiently.

3. Memory

Memory plays a crucial role in IoT devices. This includes program memory (e.g., flash memory) and data memory (e.g., RAM). Assembly programmers must manage memory resources carefully to ensure optimal performance and resource utilization.

4. Communication Interfaces

IoT devices often require communication interfaces to connect with other devices or the cloud. This may include UART, SPI, I2C, or wireless protocols like Wi-Fi or Bluetooth. Assembly code can be used to implement communication protocols efficiently.

5. Low-Power Considerations

Many IoT devices operate on battery power, making power efficiency a top priority. Assembly language programming allows developers to minimize power consumption by controlling the device's sleep modes and power states.

6. Real-Time Requirements

Some IoT applications demand real-time responsiveness, such as industrial automation or medical devices. Assembly language programming can meet these stringent timing requirements by reducing code overhead.

7. Firmware Development

IoT devices rely on firmware, which is a combination of software and hardware-specific code. Assembly language is well-suited for writing firmware due to its low-level access to hardware resources.

In the subsequent sections of this chapter, we will delve into specific aspects of assembly language programming for IoT devices. This will include coding examples, optimization techniques, and considerations for developing efficient and reliable IoT software. Whether you're working on a small sensor node or a more powerful IoT gateway, understanding assembly language can help you unlock the full potential of these connected devices.

Section 13.2: Low-Power and Energy-Efficient Coding

Efficient power management is a critical consideration in IoT devices, as many of them rely on battery power or must operate in remote locations for extended periods. Low-power coding practices are essential to prolong battery life and ensure the device's reliability. In this section, we will explore strategies for writing energy-efficient assembly code for IoT devices.

1. Idle States and Sleep Modes

One of the fundamental techniques for conserving power is to put the device into low-power states during idle periods. Modern microcontrollers offer various sleep modes that disable or reduce the power to non-essential components while keeping essential functionality active. Assembly code can be used to control the entry and exit from these low-power states efficiently.

```
; Entering sleep mode in AVR Assembly (ATmega series)
cli             ; Disable interrupts
sleep           ; Enter sleep mode
; The device will wake up upon an interrupt or specific event
sei             ; Re-enable interrupts upon wake-up
```

2. Clock Management

Reducing the clock frequency of the microcontroller when full processing power is not required can significantly reduce power consumption. Assembly code can control the clock settings to adapt to the current workload.

```
; Reducing clock frequency in MSP430 Assembly
bic.b #SCG0, &BCSCTL3   ; Clear SCG0 to reduce the DCO frequency
```

3. Peripheral Management

IoT devices often use various peripherals like sensors, communication modules, and timers. Turning off or putting these peripherals into low-power states when not in use is vital for conserving energy. Assembly code can manage these peripherals effectively.

```
; Disabling unused peripherals in ARM Cortex-M Assembly (STM32)
ldr r0, =RCC_APB1ENR
mov r1, #0x00020000    ; Bit for the specific peripheral
str r1, [r0, #0]       ; Clear the bit to disable the peripheral
```

4. Data Transmission Optimization

Efficient data transmission can help minimize the time communication modules are active, reducing power consumption. Assembly code can optimize data packet formatting and transmission protocols to reduce overhead.

5. Efficient Algorithms

Choosing energy-efficient algorithms and data structures is critical. For example, selecting algorithms with lower time and space complexity can reduce the processing workload and, consequently, power consumption.

6. Interrupt Handling

Handling interrupts efficiently is crucial, as frequent wake-ups due to poorly managed interrupts can drain the battery quickly. Assembly code can implement interrupt handlers that minimize processing time and return to sleep mode promptly.

```
; Example interrupt handler in AVR Assembly (ATmega series)
my_interrupt_handler:
  ; Process the interrupt
  ...
  reti   ; Return from interrupt
```

7. Hardware Modules for Power Monitoring

Some microcontrollers offer built-in hardware modules for power monitoring and profiling. Assembly code can utilize these modules to gather data on power consumption and identify areas for optimization.

By incorporating these low-power coding practices into assembly language programming, developers can create energy-efficient IoT applications that can operate for extended periods on limited power sources. These techniques are crucial for IoT devices deployed in remote or battery-powered environments, where power efficiency is paramount.

Section 13.3: IoT Communication Protocols

IoT devices are designed to communicate with other devices or systems to exchange data and perform various tasks. Choosing the right communication protocol is essential to ensure seamless interaction between IoT devices and their associated networks or platforms. In this section, we will explore common IoT communication protocols and discuss their characteristics and use cases.

1. Wi-Fi (802.11x)

Wi-Fi is a widely adopted wireless communication protocol that allows IoT devices to connect to local area networks (LANs) and the internet. It offers high data rates and is suitable for applications requiring real-time data transmission. IoT devices equipped with Wi-Fi modules can directly connect to existing Wi-Fi networks or act as access points.

```python
# Example code for connecting to Wi-Fi network in Python
import network

wifi = network.WLAN(network.STA_IF)
wifi.active(True)
wifi.connect('SSID', 'password')
```

Use Cases: Home automation, smart appliances, industrial automation.

2. Bluetooth (Classic and Low Energy)

Bluetooth is a short-range wireless communication protocol that is commonly used for connecting IoT devices to smartphones, tablets, and other peripherals. Bluetooth Low Energy (BLE) is particularly suitable for low-power IoT applications due to its energy-efficient characteristics.

```arduino
// Example code for Bluetooth communication in Arduino
#include <BLEDevice.h>

BLEServer *pServer;
BLEService *pService;
BLECharacteristic *pCharacteristic;

// Initialize BLE
BLEDevice::init("MyDevice");
```

Use Cases: Wearables, healthcare monitoring, proximity-based applications.

3. Zigbee

Zigbee is a low-power, low-data-rate wireless communication protocol designed for IoT and home automation applications. It operates on the IEEE 802.15.4 standard and is known for its mesh networking capabilities, making it suitable for applications with many interconnected devices.

```
// Example code for Zigbee communication in Zigbee API
#include <ZigbeeAPI.h>

ZigbeeDevice device;
device.initialize();
```

Use Cases: Smart lighting, home energy management, industrial control systems.

4. LoRaWAN

LoRaWAN (Long Range Wide Area Network) is a low-power, long-range wireless communication protocol designed for IoT devices that need to transmit data over extended distances. It is well-suited for applications in remote or outdoor environments.

```
# Example code for LoRaWAN communication in Python
from network import LoRa

lora = LoRa(mode=LoRa.LORAWAN)
lora.join(activation=LoRa.OTAA, auth=(app_eui, app_key), timeout=0)
```

Use Cases: Agriculture, environmental monitoring, smart cities.

5. MQTT (Message Queuing Telemetry Transport)

MQTT is a lightweight publish-subscribe messaging protocol designed for efficient communication between IoT devices and servers or cloud platforms. It minimizes the overhead of communication, making it suitable for resource-constrained IoT devices.

```
// Example code for MQTT communication in JavaScript
const mqtt = require('mqtt');
const client = mqtt.connect('mqtt://broker.example.com');

client.on('connect', () => {
  client.subscribe('iot/devices/mydevice');
});

client.on('message', (topic, message) => {
  console.log(`Received message on topic ${topic}: ${message.toString()}`);
});
```

Use Cases: IoT data telemetry, sensor networks, home automation.

6. CoAP (Constrained Application Protocol)

CoAP is a lightweight, RESTful application protocol designed for resource-constrained IoT devices. It is suitable for applications that require simple and efficient communication patterns, such as querying sensor data.

```c
// Example code for CoAP communication in C
#include <coap.h>

coap_context_t *ctx = coap_new_context(NULL);

coap_uri_t uri;
coap_uri_parse("coap://example.com/resource", &uri);
```

Use Cases: Smart agriculture, industrial monitoring, smart building automation.

7. HTTP/HTTPS

HTTP/HTTPS are widely used communication protocols for IoT devices that need to interact with web services or cloud platforms. They are suitable for IoT applications that require standard web-based communication.

```python
# Example code for HTTP communication in Python
import requests

response = requests.get('https://api.example.com/data')
print(response.text)
```

Use Cases: Cloud integration, remote monitoring, web-based control interfaces.

Choosing the appropriate communication protocol for your IoT project depends on factors such as range, power consumption, data rate, and compatibility with existing infrastructure. By selecting the right protocol, you can ensure that your IoT devices can communicate effectively with other devices and systems, enabling the desired functionality and data exchange.

Section 13.4: Sensor Integration

In the world of IoT, sensors play a pivotal role in collecting data from the physical environment. These sensors can measure a wide range of parameters such as temperature, humidity, pressure, motion, light, and more. In this section, we'll explore the integration of sensors into IoT devices and how to interface with them to collect valuable data.

Sensor Types and Selection

Choosing the right sensor for your IoT project is crucial, as it directly impacts the type of data you can collect. Here are some common sensor types:

1. **Temperature Sensors:** These sensors measure temperature variations in the environment. Examples include thermistors, infrared temperature sensors, and digital temperature sensors like the DHT series.

2. **Humidity Sensors:** Humidity sensors, such as the DHT22, measure the amount of moisture in the air.

3. **Light Sensors:** Light sensors detect light levels, enabling applications like automatic lighting control or outdoor light intensity monitoring.

4. **Proximity Sensors:** These sensors can detect the presence or absence of an object within a certain range, making them useful for applications like automated doors or proximity detection.

5. **Motion Sensors:** Motion sensors, including passive infrared (PIR) sensors, detect movement and are commonly used in security systems.

6. **Pressure Sensors:** Pressure sensors measure air or fluid pressure and find applications in weather monitoring, altitude measurement, and more.

7. **Gas Sensors:** Gas sensors can detect specific gases like carbon dioxide (CO_2), carbon monoxide (CO), or methane (CH_4), making them essential for environmental monitoring and safety.

8. **Sound Sensors:** These sensors can capture sound or vibration data and are useful in applications like noise monitoring or acoustic analysis.

Sensor Interface and Data Acquisition

IoT devices need the ability to interface with sensors and collect data. Microcontrollers, such as Arduino, Raspberry Pi, or ESP8266/ESP32, are commonly used for this purpose. Most sensors communicate via analog voltage levels or digital interfaces like I2C, SPI, or UART.

Let's take an example of reading data from a DHT22 temperature and humidity sensor using a Raspberry Pi and Python:

```python
import Adafruit_DHT

# Sensor type and GPIO pin configuration
sensor = Adafruit_DHT.DHT22
pin = 4

# Attempt to read data from the sensor
humidity, temperature = Adafruit_DHT.read_retry(sensor, pin)

if humidity is not None and temperature is not None:
    print(f'Temperature: {temperature:.2f}°C, Humidity: {humidity:.2f}%')
else:
    print('Failed to retrieve data from the sensor.')
```

Data Processing and Analysis

Once data is collected from sensors, it may require processing or analysis before being sent to a central server or cloud platform. This processing can include data smoothing, calibration, or converting raw sensor values into meaningful units.

For example, you might need to convert analog sensor readings into temperature values using appropriate formulas or perform outlier detection to remove erroneous data points.

Connectivity and Data Transmission

Finally, IoT devices need a means of transmitting sensor data to a central server or cloud service. Communication protocols discussed in previous sections, such as Wi-Fi, Bluetooth, LoRaWAN, MQTT, or HTTP, can be used to achieve this. The choice of protocol depends on factors like range, power consumption, and network infrastructure.

In summary, sensor integration is a fundamental aspect of IoT development. Choosing the right sensors, interfacing them with microcontrollers, processing the data, and transmitting it using suitable communication protocols are key steps in building effective IoT systems. The specific sensors and techniques you choose will depend on your project's requirements and objectives.

Section 13.5: Developing IoT Solutions in Assembly

Developing IoT solutions in assembly language can be a challenging yet rewarding endeavor. While high-level languages are commonly used in IoT development due to their ease of use, memory efficiency, and portability, there are cases where assembly language can offer distinct advantages. In this section, we'll explore scenarios where using assembly in IoT projects can be beneficial and provide insights into its practical application.

Real-Time and Low-Level Control

One of the primary reasons to consider assembly language in IoT is for real-time and low-level control. In certain applications, especially those that require precise timing or interaction with hardware peripherals, assembly can provide the fine-grained control necessary to meet stringent requirements.

For instance, in a microcontroller-based IoT device that controls a motor or reads data from a sensor with tight timing constraints, assembly language can be employed to optimize code execution and achieve high precision.

Firmware Development for Resource-Constrained Devices

IoT devices often run on resource-constrained hardware, such as microcontrollers with limited memory and processing power. In such cases, assembly language can help create efficient and compact firmware. By hand-optimizing critical parts of the code, developers can reduce memory usage and improve the device's overall performance.

However, it's essential to strike a balance between code efficiency and development time. Assembly development can be time-consuming, and optimizations should focus on areas that genuinely benefit from low-level control.

Portability Across Architectures

One potential drawback of using assembly in IoT is its lack of portability. Code written in assembly for one architecture may not run on another. However, some assembly languages, like ARM assembly, are widely used in IoT devices, making it possible to reuse code across a range of ARM-based microcontrollers.

When using assembly for IoT, consider the long-term implications and whether the benefits of code efficiency outweigh the challenges of potential platform lock-in.

Security and Trustworthiness

Security is a paramount concern in IoT, particularly for applications involving critical infrastructure or sensitive data. Assembly code can enhance security by reducing the attack surface and eliminating vulnerabilities introduced by higher-level languages and libraries. Developers can meticulously review and audit assembly code for potential security flaws.

However, the effectiveness of assembly-based security depends on the expertise of the developers and their ability to identify and mitigate risks effectively.

Example: Assembly Language for IoT

Let's consider a simple example of using assembly language for IoT. Suppose you have an IoT device that monitors environmental parameters and transmits data over a low-power wireless protocol like LoRaWAN. The device needs to maximize battery life and operate reliably in remote locations.

In this scenario, you might use assembly language to:

1. Optimize the power management routines for efficient use of the device's energy resources.
2. Implement a custom, minimalistic LoRaWAN stack tailored to the specific requirements of the application.
3. Minimize the device's sleep current by controlling hardware peripherals directly in assembly code.

By doing so, you can achieve extended battery life and ensure the device operates reliably in remote and challenging environments.

In conclusion, while assembly language development for IoT presents challenges and demands expertise, it can be a valuable tool in specific scenarios where real-time control, resource efficiency, and security are critical. Developers should carefully evaluate the trade-offs between code efficiency and development complexity when considering assembly for IoT projects.

Chapter 14: Assembly Language for Cryptography

Section 14.1: Cryptographic Concepts

Cryptography plays a vital role in ensuring the security and privacy of digital communications, data storage, and various online transactions. In this section, we'll delve into the fundamental cryptographic concepts that underpin the field and explore how assembly language can be applied to cryptographic tasks.

The Importance of Cryptography

Cryptography is the science of securing information by transforming it into an unreadable format, known as ciphertext, using mathematical algorithms and secret keys. The primary objectives of cryptography are:

1. **Confidentiality:** Ensuring that unauthorized parties cannot read the protected information.
2. **Integrity:** Verifying that the data has not been tampered with during transmission or storage.
3. **Authentication:** Confirming the identity of communicating parties.
4. **Non-repudiation:** Preventing parties from denying their actions or transactions.

Cryptography is essential for safeguarding sensitive data, such as financial transactions, personal information, and classified government communications.

Symmetric vs. Asymmetric Cryptography

Two fundamental categories of cryptographic algorithms exist: symmetric and asymmetric.

Symmetric Cryptography

Symmetric cryptography, also known as secret-key cryptography, employs a single secret key for both encryption and decryption. The same key is used to lock (encrypt) and unlock (decrypt) the information. Common symmetric algorithms include AES (Advanced Encryption Standard) and DES (Data Encryption Standard).

Symmetric cryptography is computationally efficient and suitable for encrypting large amounts of data quickly. However, a key distribution challenge exists since both parties need to possess the secret key.

Asymmetric Cryptography

Asymmetric cryptography, also called public-key cryptography, uses a pair of keys: a public key for encryption and a private key for decryption. Data encrypted with the public key can only be decrypted with the corresponding private key and vice versa. The RSA and ECC (Elliptic Curve Cryptography) algorithms are widely used asymmetric cryptography methods.

Asymmetric cryptography addresses the key distribution problem since public keys can be freely shared, while private keys remain secret. This makes it suitable for secure communications and digital signatures. However, it is computationally more intensive than symmetric cryptography.

Hash Functions

Hash functions are a critical component of modern cryptography. They take an input (or message) and produce a fixed-size output, known as a hash value or digest. Hash functions have several essential properties:

1. **Deterministic:** The same input will always produce the same hash value.
2. **Fast Computation:** Hash functions are designed to be computed quickly.
3. **Pre-image Resistance:** Given a hash value, it should be computationally infeasible to reverse the process and determine the original input.
4. **Collision Resistance:** It should be unlikely that two different inputs produce the same hash value.

Hash functions are used in various cryptographic applications, such as password storage, digital signatures, and data integrity verification.

Practical Application of Assembly in Cryptography

Assembly language is well-suited for cryptographic implementations due to its low-level control over hardware and computational efficiency. Cryptographic libraries and protocols often include assembly code optimized for specific architectures to maximize performance and security.

Developing cryptographic algorithms in assembly requires a deep understanding of both the algorithm and the target architecture. Assembly programmers must consider factors like data representation, memory management, and side-channel attacks when implementing cryptographic operations.

In this chapter, we'll explore how assembly language can be used to implement cryptographic algorithms, secure key management, and build cryptographic libraries. We'll also delve into the challenges and best practices for secure assembly programming in the context of cryptography.

Section 14.2: Encryption and Decryption Algorithms

In the realm of cryptography, encryption and decryption algorithms form the backbone of securing information. These algorithms determine how data is transformed into ciphertext for secure transmission and how it is later transformed back into its original form for use.

Symmetric encryption relies on a single secret key for both encryption and decryption. Here are some commonly used symmetric encryption algorithms:

1. **AES (Advanced Encryption Standard):** AES is a widely adopted symmetric encryption algorithm known for its security and efficiency. It operates on blocks of data and supports key lengths of 128, 192, and 256 bits.

2. **DES (Data Encryption Standard):** DES was one of the earliest symmetric encryption algorithms. It uses a 56-bit key and operates on 64-bit blocks of data. While it's no longer considered secure against modern attacks, it laid the foundation for subsequent encryption algorithms.

3. **3DES (Triple DES):** 3DES is a more secure variant of DES. It applies DES encryption three times with different keys, making it computationally intensive but still secure.

4. **RC4 (Rivest Cipher 4):** RC4 is a stream cipher known for its simplicity and speed. It's often used in wireless and internet security protocols like WEP and WPA.

Symmetric encryption algorithms are fast and efficient, making them suitable for encrypting data in bulk. However, the challenge lies in securely sharing the secret key between communicating parties.

Asymmetric Encryption Algorithms

Asymmetric encryption, also known as public-key encryption, employs a pair of keys: a public key for encryption and a private key for decryption. This approach solves the key distribution problem faced by symmetric encryption. Common asymmetric encryption algorithms include:

1. **RSA (Rivest-Shamir-Adleman):** RSA is widely used for secure communications and digital signatures. It relies on the difficulty of factoring large composite numbers to ensure security.

2. **DSA (Digital Signature Algorithm):** DSA is used for digital signatures and authentication. It is closely related to the Diffie-Hellman key exchange algorithm.

3. **ECC (Elliptic Curve Cryptography):** ECC is known for its strong security with relatively short key lengths, making it computationally efficient. It's often used in resource-constrained environments.

Asymmetric encryption is computationally more intensive than symmetric encryption, making it suitable for tasks like secure key exchange and digital signatures. It's commonly used in securing web communications (HTTPS), email encryption, and secure shell (SSH) connections.

Hybrid Encryption

To combine the advantages of both symmetric and asymmetric encryption, a common practice is to use hybrid encryption. In this approach, a symmetric key is generated for each session, used for encrypting the actual data, and then encrypted with the recipient's public key. This allows for efficient bulk data encryption using symmetric cryptography while securely sharing the symmetric key using asymmetric cryptography.

Hybrid encryption is widely used in secure communications and data protection applications.

Assembly Language and Encryption

Assembly language can be instrumental in implementing encryption and decryption algorithms efficiently. The fine-grained control over hardware resources and instruction-level optimization can lead to highly performant cryptographic implementations.

However, it's important to note that implementing encryption algorithms in assembly requires a deep understanding of both the algorithm and the target architecture. Mistakes can lead to vulnerabilities, so thorough testing and validation are crucial in cryptographic software development.

In the upcoming sections of this chapter, we will explore practical examples of implementing encryption and decryption algorithms in assembly language, highlighting the key considerations for secure and efficient implementations.

Section 14.3: Secure Key Management

Effective key management is a fundamental aspect of cryptographic systems. Regardless of how strong your encryption algorithm is, if the keys are not properly managed and secured, the entire system can be compromised. In this section, we will delve into the principles and practices of secure key management.

Key Generation

The first step in key management is key generation. Keys must be generated using strong, random processes to ensure unpredictability. Secure key generation typically involves the following:

- **Randomness:** Keys should be generated from a source of true randomness. Pseudorandom number generators (PRNGs) should not be used for generating cryptographic keys as they are deterministic and predictable.

- **Key Length:** Longer keys are generally more secure. The appropriate key length depends on the encryption algorithm being used and the specific security requirements. For example, AES-256 uses 256-bit keys.

- **Key Storage:** Keys must be stored securely, preferably in hardware security modules (HSMs) or trusted execution environments (TEEs) that protect against physical and software-based attacks.

Key distribution is a critical challenge in cryptography, especially in asymmetric encryption. Secure key exchange mechanisms are needed to ensure that keys are shared only between trusted parties. Common methods include:

- **Diffie-Hellman Key Exchange:** This method allows two parties to generate a shared secret over an insecure communication channel without actually transmitting the secret itself. It's commonly used in securing internet communications (e.g., TLS/SSL).

- **Public Key Infrastructure (PKI):** PKI systems use digital certificates to verify the authenticity of public keys. Certificate authorities (CAs) play a key role in issuing and verifying these certificates.

- **Key Agreement Protocols:** Protocols like ECDH (Elliptic Curve Diffie-Hellman) enable secure key exchange using asymmetric cryptography.

Storing keys securely is crucial to prevent unauthorized access. Keys should never be stored in plaintext, especially in software or configuration files. Instead, consider these practices:

- **Hardware Security Modules (HSMs):** HSMs are dedicated hardware devices designed to safeguard cryptographic keys. They provide a high level of protection against physical and software-based attacks.

- **Secure Key Vaults:** Cloud-based secure key vaults like AWS Key Management Service (KMS) or Azure Key Vault offer secure key storage and management services.

- **Key Derivation:** Use key derivation functions (KDFs) to derive cryptographic keys from master keys or passwords. This adds an extra layer of security by ensuring that the actual encryption keys are not exposed.

Keys should not remain static indefinitely. Regular key rotation is essential to mitigate the impact of key compromise. Key rotation involves generating new keys and updating cryptographic configurations. The old keys should be securely retired.

In the event of key loss or compromise, a key backup and recovery mechanism is essential. This typically involves securely storing copies of keys in separate physical locations or utilizing split knowledge mechanisms where multiple parties must collaborate to recover keys.

Cryptographic Erasure

When keys are no longer needed, they should be securely erased to prevent any potential recovery. This process, called cryptographic erasure or key zeroization, ensures that no traces of the key remain in memory or storage.

Security Policies and Procedures

Finally, organizations should establish clear security policies and procedures for key management. This includes defining who has access to keys, under what circumstances keys can be accessed, and how key-related incidents are handled.

In summary, secure key management is a critical component of cryptographic systems. Keys should be generated and stored with the utmost care, and key distribution, rotation, backup, and erasure should be well-defined processes. Adhering to these practices is essential for maintaining the confidentiality and integrity of sensitive data.

Section 14.4: Cryptographic Libraries in Assembly

Cryptographic libraries play a pivotal role in implementing secure cryptographic algorithms and protocols. They provide a set of functions and routines that allow developers to perform cryptographic operations without delving into the low-level details of the algorithms. In this section, we'll explore the importance of cryptographic libraries and discuss their use in assembly language programming.

The Role of Cryptographic Libraries

1. **Abstraction and Simplification:** Cryptographic libraries abstract away the intricate details of cryptographic algorithms, making it easier for developers to use encryption and decryption in their applications. This abstraction simplifies the implementation process and reduces the risk of errors.

2. **Security Assurance:** Reputable cryptographic libraries are thoroughly tested and vetted for security vulnerabilities. Using a trusted library helps ensure that cryptographic operations are performed correctly and securely.

3. **Performance Optimization:** Many cryptographic libraries are optimized for specific hardware platforms, including assembly language implementations. This can result in significant performance improvements compared to custom, non-optimized implementations.

Cryptographic Libraries in Assembly

When working with assembly language, developers may need to interface with cryptographic libraries to perform encryption, decryption, and other security-related operations. Here are some key considerations:

1. **Library Selection:** Choose a cryptographic library that is compatible with your assembly language development environment and target architecture. Libraries like OpenSSL and libsodium offer assembly language bindings for various platforms.

2. **Function Calls:** To use a cryptographic library in assembly, you'll typically make function calls to the library's API. These function calls are similar to regular assembly function calls, but they involve passing arguments and retrieving results in accordance with the library's documentation.

3. **Register Usage:** Pay attention to the calling conventions and register usage expected by the library. You may need to save and restore registers as necessary to avoid conflicts with library code.

4. **Error Handling:** Most cryptographic libraries provide error handling mechanisms to report issues during cryptographic operations. Ensure that you check error codes and handle errors appropriately in your assembly code.

5. **Memory Management:** Cryptographic operations often involve working with buffers and memory allocation. Be mindful of memory management to prevent buffer overflows and memory leaks.

6. **Endianness:** Some cryptographic libraries may require you to handle endianness (byte order) considerations, especially when interfacing with external systems or network protocols.

Example Pseudocode

Here's a simplified pseudocode example demonstrating how you might use a cryptographic library in assembly to perform encryption:

```
; Load plaintext and key into registers
load plaintext, %r1
load key, %r2

; Call the library's encryption function
call crypto_encrypt, %r1, %r2, %r3

; Check for errors
cmp %r3, 0
jne error_handling

; Encrypted data is now in %r1
; Continue with further processing
```

In this example, we load plaintext and a cryptographic key into registers, call the `crypto_encrypt` function from the library, and handle errors if the function returns a non-zero value.

Conclusion

Cryptographic libraries are invaluable tools for implementing secure cryptographic functionality in assembly language programs. They provide a level of abstraction, security assurance, and performance optimization that can significantly simplify the development process and improve the security of your applications. When working with these libraries, be sure to follow the library's documentation and guidelines for assembly language integration.

Section 14.5: Building Secure Systems with Assembly

Building secure systems with assembly language involves a deep understanding of both low-level programming and security principles. In this section, we'll explore the key considerations and best practices for developing secure systems in assembly.

Security by Design

1. **Threat Modeling:** Begin by identifying potential threats and attack vectors specific to your system. Consider factors like data privacy, data integrity, and system availability.

2. **Minimize Attack Surface:** Reduce the attack surface by eliminating unnecessary features, limiting system privileges, and applying the principle of least privilege.

3. **Secure Boot Process:** Implement a secure boot process to ensure that only trusted code is executed during system startup. This often involves cryptographic verification of bootloaders and firmware.

Memory Safety

4. **Buffer Overflow Prevention:** Buffer overflows are a common source of vulnerabilities. Use techniques like bounds checking and stack canaries to prevent these vulnerabilities.

5. **Secure Coding Practices:** Follow secure coding practices, such as input validation and output sanitization, to mitigate common vulnerabilities like SQL injection and cross-site scripting (XSS).

6. **Memory Management:** Be vigilant with memory management. Use safe memory allocation and deallocation practices to prevent memory leaks and buffer overflows.

Data Encryption

7. **Data Encryption:** Implement strong encryption algorithms to protect sensitive data at rest and in transit. Use cryptographic libraries to ensure proper encryption and decryption processes.

8. **Secure Key Management:** Develop robust key management procedures to safeguard encryption keys. Keys should be stored securely and regularly rotated.

Access Control

9. **Access Control:** Enforce access control mechanisms to restrict unauthorized access to resources and functionalities. Implement role-based access control (RBAC) or mandatory access control (MAC) where applicable.

10. **Authentication and Authorization:** Implement secure authentication mechanisms, such as multi-factor authentication (MFA), and authorization checks to ensure that users and processes have the necessary permissions.

Error Handling

11. **Error Handling:** Handle errors gracefully to prevent information leakage. Avoid exposing sensitive system details in error messages.

12. **Logging and Monitoring:** Implement robust logging and monitoring to detect and respond to security incidents promptly. Log files should be protected against unauthorized access.

Security Testing

13. **Security Testing:** Conduct thorough security testing, including penetration testing and code reviews, to identify vulnerabilities and weaknesses in your system.

Firmware and Hardware Security

14. **Firmware Security:** If your system includes firmware or microcontrollers, secure them against tampering and unauthorized updates. Consider using secure boot and hardware-based security features.

Continuous Vigilance

15. **Patch Management:** Stay vigilant about security updates and patches. Regularly update your system's software and libraries to address known vulnerabilities.

16. **Security Awareness:** Train developers, administrators, and users in security best practices to create a security-aware culture.

Regulatory Compliance

17. **Compliance:** Depending on your application, you may need to adhere to industry-specific security standards and regulations. Ensure compliance with standards like ISO 27001, HIPAA, or GDPR, where applicable.

Building secure systems in assembly is a challenging but essential task, especially for applications that require the highest levels of security. By incorporating these principles and practices into your assembly language development process, you can create robust and resilient systems that protect against a wide range of threats and vulnerabilities. Remember that security is an ongoing process, and it requires continuous effort to stay ahead of emerging threats.

Chapter 15: Assembly Language for Multimedia Processing

Section 15.1: Multimedia Data Formats

Multimedia processing in assembly language involves working with various data formats that encompass audio, video, and image data. To efficiently process multimedia data, it is essential to understand these formats and how they are structured. In this section, we'll delve into the basics of multimedia data formats and their significance in assembly programming.

Understanding Multimedia Data

Multimedia data comprises a combination of audio, video, or image elements, often synchronized to create a cohesive user experience. Before diving into specific formats, let's explore some common characteristics of multimedia data:

1. **Data Compression**: Multimedia data is often compressed to reduce storage space and bandwidth requirements. Compression techniques like lossless and lossy compression are employed to strike a balance between quality and size.

2. **Container Formats**: Multimedia files often use container formats (e.g., MP4, AVI, MKV) to encapsulate audio, video, and metadata into a single file. These formats can store data encoded in various codecs.

3. **Codecs**: Codecs (Coder-Decoder) are used to encode and decode audio and video data. Popular video codecs include H.264 and VP9, while audio codecs like AAC and MP3 are widely used.

4. **Metadata**: Multimedia files contain metadata such as title, author, and timestamp. This metadata is crucial for organizing and displaying multimedia content.

Audio Data Formats

Audio data in multimedia typically comes in formats like WAV, MP3, AAC, and FLAC. Each format has its characteristics and compression algorithms. For example, WAV files are uncompressed, providing high-quality audio but consuming more storage space. MP3 and AAC, on the other hand, use lossy compression to achieve smaller file sizes at the cost of some audio quality.

Video Data Formats

Video data formats include AVI, MP4, MKV, and more. These formats can store video streams using different codecs. For example, an MP4 file can contain video encoded with H.264 and audio encoded with AAC. Understanding how to extract and manipulate video frames and audio samples within these formats is vital for multimedia processing.

Image Data Formats

Image data formats encompass popular formats like JPEG, PNG, BMP, and GIF. These formats define how images are stored, compressed, and encoded. JPEG, known for its lossy compression, is widely used for photographs, while PNG offers lossless compression and is suitable for images with transparency.

Challenges in Multimedia Processing

Processing multimedia data in assembly language presents several challenges:

- **Data Parsing**: Efficiently parsing multimedia files to extract audio, video, and metadata requires careful handling of file structures and headers.

- **Codec Implementation**: Implementing codecs for audio and video compression/decompression demands a deep understanding of compression algorithms and bitwise operations.

- **Real-Time Processing**: Multimedia applications often require real-time processing to maintain synchronization between audio and video elements, making timing critical.

- **Optimization**: Multimedia processing can be computationally intensive. Assembly language offers optimization opportunities to boost performance.

In the subsequent sections of this chapter, we will explore techniques for processing multimedia data, including audio and video codecs, image processing algorithms, and real-time multimedia applications in assembly language.

Section 15.2: Audio and Video Codecs

Audio and video codecs are essential components of multimedia processing. Codecs play a crucial role in encoding and decoding audio and video data, enabling efficient storage and transmission of multimedia content. In this section, we will explore the fundamentals of audio and video codecs and how they can be implemented or utilized in assembly language.

Understanding Codecs

A codec (Coder-Decoder) is a software or hardware component responsible for compressing (encoding) and decompressing (decoding) multimedia data. Codecs are essential because they reduce the size of audio and video files, making them more manageable for storage and transmission. Here are some key aspects of codecs:

1. **Compression**: Codecs employ compression techniques to reduce the size of multimedia data. There are two main types of compression:

- **Lossless Compression**: This type of compression reduces file size without any loss in quality. It is used for formats where quality preservation is critical, like text or certain image formats.
- **Lossy Compression**: Lossy compression sacrifices some quality to achieve more significant file size reduction. It is commonly used for audio and video formats.

2. **Encoding**: Encoding refers to the process of converting raw audio or video data into a compressed format. During encoding, codecs apply algorithms that identify redundancies and remove or reduce them.

3. **Decoding**: Decoding is the reverse process of encoding. It involves taking the compressed data and restoring it to its original, uncompressed form for playback or editing.

Audio Codecs

Audio codecs are responsible for compressing and decompressing audio data. Some well-known audio codecs include:

- **MP3 (MPEG-1 Audio Layer III)**: MP3 is a popular lossy audio codec known for its efficient compression. It achieves high compression ratios by discarding some audio data that the human ear is less sensitive to.

- **AAC (Advanced Audio Coding)**: AAC is another lossy audio codec widely used for high-quality audio. It is commonly associated with formats like M4A (used by Apple) and MP4.

- **FLAC (Free Lossless Audio Codec)**: Unlike the lossy codecs mentioned above, FLAC is a lossless codec that retains audio quality but results in larger file sizes. It is favored for archival and high-fidelity audio.

Video Codecs

Video codecs are designed to compress and decompress video data efficiently. Some prominent video codecs include:

- **H.264 (Advanced Video Coding, AVC)**: H.264 is a widely used video codec known for its high compression efficiency. It is commonly used for video streaming, video conferencing, and more.

- **VP9**: Developed by Google, VP9 is an open-source video codec that offers competitive compression ratios with H.264 while maintaining good video quality.

- **HEVC (High-Efficiency Video Coding, H.265)**: HEVC is designed to provide better compression than H.264, making it suitable for 4K and higher-resolution video content.

Implementing audio and video codecs in assembly language is a complex task that requires in-depth knowledge of compression algorithms, bitwise operations, and the specifics of the codec standards. Assembly language's low-level control over hardware resources can be advantageous for optimization.

Typically, codec implementations involve:

- Bit-level manipulation for encoding and decoding.
- Transformations like discrete cosine transforms (DCT) or discrete wavelet transforms (DWT) for video and audio data.
- Entropy coding techniques such as Huffman coding or arithmetic coding.
- Profound understanding of the codec's specifications and standards.

Efficient codec implementations in assembly can lead to high-performance multimedia processing, making assembly language a valuable tool in multimedia applications. However, codec development is a specialized field, and many projects leverage existing codec libraries for their multimedia processing needs.

In the subsequent sections, we will explore more about multimedia processing techniques and assembly language's role in this domain.

Section 15.3: Image Processing Algorithms

Image processing is a fundamental aspect of multimedia processing that involves manipulating and enhancing digital images to achieve specific goals. In this section, we will delve into image processing algorithms and how assembly language can be used for efficient image processing.

Basic Image Processing Operations

Image processing encompasses a wide range of operations, from simple manipulations to complex transformations. Some basic image processing operations include:

1. **Image Enhancement**: Techniques to improve image quality, such as adjusting brightness, contrast, and color balance.

2. **Image Filtering**: Convolution-based operations that apply filters (e.g., blurring, sharpening) to highlight or remove certain features.

3. **Image Thresholding**: The process of separating objects or features from the background by setting a threshold.

4. **Image Rotation and Scaling**: Transformations that change the orientation and size of an image.

5. **Image Compression**: Reducing the size of images to save storage space or enable efficient transmission.

Assembly language can be a powerful choice for implementing image processing algorithms due to its low-level control over hardware resources. While higher-level programming languages are commonly used for image processing, assembly language can provide optimizations for critical operations, especially in real-time or resource-constrained environments.

Here are some aspects to consider when using assembly language for image processing:

1. **Performance Optimization**: Assembly language allows for fine-grained control over processor registers and operations, enabling performance optimizations like loop unrolling, vectorization, and parallelism.

2. **Memory Access**: Efficient memory access patterns are crucial in image processing. Assembly code can be optimized to minimize memory latency and maximize cache utilization.

3. **Bitwise Operations**: Image processing often involves bitwise operations to manipulate individual pixels or image regions. Assembly excels in performing bitwise operations efficiently.

4. **Custom Implementations**: Assembly language allows you to create custom implementations of image processing algorithms tailored to your specific requirements.

5. **Integration with Other Languages**: Assembly code can be integrated with higher-level languages like C or C++ to harness the benefits of both low-level and high-level programming.

One common image processing operation is convolution filtering, which applies a kernel (matrix) to an image to perform operations like blurring or edge detection. Here's a simplified assembly-like pseudocode for a convolution operation:

```
for each pixel in the image:
    result = 0
    for each kernel element:
        result += pixel_value * kernel_element
    output_pixel = result
```

In practice, implementing convolution in assembly language involves optimizing the inner loop for efficiency, considering factors like loop unrolling and cache utilization.

While assembly language can be used for image processing, many libraries and frameworks in higher-level languages (e.g., OpenCV in C/C++, Pillow in Python) provide efficient implementations of various image processing algorithms. These libraries are often preferred for their ease of use and wide range of functionalities.

In the upcoming sections, we will explore more advanced image processing techniques and their application in assembly language, as well as their relevance in multimedia processing applications.

Section 15.4: Multimedia Streaming

Multimedia streaming refers to the continuous delivery of multimedia content, such as audio and video, over a network in real-time. This section explores the concept of multimedia streaming, its importance in various applications, and how assembly language can play a role in optimizing multimedia streaming systems.

Understanding Multimedia Streaming

Multimedia streaming is a technology that enables users to consume multimedia content without downloading the entire file beforehand. Instead, the content is delivered in a continuous stream, allowing users to watch or listen to it as it arrives. Streaming is widely used for various types of content, including:

- **Video Streaming**: Platforms like YouTube, Netflix, and live streaming services deliver video content in real-time.

- **Audio Streaming**: Services like Spotify and Apple Music stream audio tracks to users' devices.

- **Live Broadcasting**: Events like sports matches, concerts, and news broadcasts are streamed live to a global audience.

- **Webinars and Conferencing**: Platforms like Zoom and WebEx use streaming for real-time communication.

Challenges in Multimedia Streaming

Multimedia streaming faces several challenges:

1. **Bandwidth and Network Quality**: Streaming quality relies on available bandwidth and network stability. Insufficient bandwidth or network interruptions can result in buffering or reduced quality.

2. **Latency**: Real-time streaming requires low latency to minimize delays between content generation and user consumption, crucial for live events and interactive applications.

3. **Compression**: Multimedia content is often compressed to reduce file size and improve streaming efficiency. Codecs (encoding/decoding algorithms) play a crucial role here.

4. **Adaptive Streaming**: Adaptive streaming techniques adjust quality based on available bandwidth, device capabilities, and network conditions to ensure a seamless viewing experience.

5. **Content Protection**: Protecting copyrighted content from piracy is essential, necessitating encryption and digital rights management (DRM) solutions.

Assembly Language in Multimedia Streaming

Assembly language can be employed in various aspects of multimedia streaming for optimization purposes:

1. **Codec Implementations**: Implementing video and audio codecs in assembly language can significantly improve encoding and decoding performance.

2. **Network Optimization**: Assembly-level optimizations can enhance network communication efficiency, reducing latency and improving streaming quality.

3. **Buffer Management**: Efficient buffer management in streaming servers and clients can be implemented using assembly language for optimal memory usage and data throughput.

4. **Encryption and DRM**: Security-related components, such as encryption and DRM, can benefit from assembly-level optimizations for better performance and protection.

Example: Video Codec Optimization

Optimizing video codecs in assembly language involves using low-level instructions to accelerate the encoding and decoding processes. For instance, SIMD (Single Instruction, Multiple Data) instructions in modern processors can be leveraged to process multiple pixels simultaneously, improving encoding and decoding speed.

```
; Pseudocode for SIMD-based video codec optimization
for each group of pixels:
    load multiple pixels into SIMD registers
    apply codec operations on the pixel group
    store the result
```

Such optimizations are crucial for delivering high-quality video streams efficiently.

In conclusion, multimedia streaming is a vital technology for delivering real-time audio and video content over networks. Assembly language can be a valuable tool for optimizing various aspects of multimedia streaming systems, from codec implementations to network communication, contributing to better performance and user experience.

Section 15.5: Real-Time Multimedia Applications in Assembly

Real-time multimedia applications require high performance and low latency to provide a seamless user experience. In this section, we'll explore how assembly language programming can be employed to develop real-time multimedia applications, such as video conferencing, audio processing, and interactive multimedia experiences.

The Need for Real-Time Performance

Real-time multimedia applications include video conferencing platforms like Zoom, online gaming with voice chat, and interactive multimedia installations in museums or theme parks. These applications demand instantaneous responses to user inputs and low latency in audio and video processing.

Assembly Language in Real-Time Multimedia

1. **Audio Processing**: Assembly language can be utilized to optimize audio processing routines, such as audio mixing, effects, and real-time audio synthesis. By carefully crafting assembly code, developers can reduce processing time and achieve minimal audio latency.

2. **Video Processing**: Video processing tasks like frame encoding, decoding, and rendering benefit from assembly-level optimizations. SIMD instructions can be employed to parallelize pixel operations, enhancing video rendering speed.

3. **Data Streaming**: Real-time multimedia applications often involve data streaming between multiple clients. Assembly language can be used to implement efficient network protocols and data compression techniques, minimizing latency and bandwidth usage.

4. **User Interface**: Even the user interface of real-time multimedia applications can be optimized using assembly language. For instance, fast and responsive UI elements can enhance the overall user experience.

Example: Real-Time Audio Processing

Consider a real-time audio processing application that applies live audio effects to a microphone input. Assembly language can optimize the core processing loop for minimum latency:

```
; Pseudocode for real-time audio processing in assembly
while application is running:
    capture audio input
    apply audio effects (e.g., reverb, equalization) using optimized assembly
code
    send processed audio to output
```

By optimizing the audio effects processing with assembly language, developers can reduce the delay between capturing audio and hearing the processed output, creating a more responsive and immersive experience.

Conclusion

Assembly language programming plays a crucial role in real-time multimedia applications by enabling developers to achieve the performance and low latency required for a seamless user experience. Whether it's optimizing audio and video processing, data streaming, or user interface elements, assembly language can help deliver real-time multimedia applications that meet the demands of today's users.

Chapter 16: Advanced Assembly Language Techniques

Section 16.1: Advanced Data Structures

In this section, we will delve into the world of advanced data structures in assembly language programming. While assembly is often associated with low-level memory manipulation, it can be used to implement sophisticated data structures efficiently. Understanding and implementing advanced data structures in assembly is valuable in scenarios where performance and memory utilization are critical.

The Role of Data Structures in Assembly

1. **Memory Efficiency**: Assembly language allows developers to fine-tune memory allocation and minimize overhead associated with high-level language data structures.

2. **Performance**: Advanced data structures can improve algorithm efficiency. For example, a well-designed hash table in assembly can lead to faster lookups compared to linear searches.

3. **Embedded Systems**: In embedded systems, where resources are limited, implementing custom data structures in assembly can help optimize memory usage and execution speed.

Implementing Advanced Data Structures

Example: Linked List

Consider implementing a linked list in assembly. While this data structure is relatively simple, it demonstrates the principles of advanced data structure design in assembly.

```
; Pseudocode for a singly linked list node in assembly
struct Node:
    value   ; Data stored in the node
    next    ; Pointer to the next node
```

The above assembly pseudo-struct defines a linked list node with two fields: value to hold the data and next to point to the next node in the list.

Example: Binary Search Tree (BST)

Implementing a binary search tree in assembly can be more complex but showcases advanced data structure design. A BST has nodes with left and right children, allowing for efficient searching.

```
; Pseudocode for a binary search tree node in assembly
struct TreeNode:
    key     ; Key value
```

```
    left     ; Pointer to the left child
    right    ; Pointer to the right child
```

1. **Memory Optimization**: Advanced data structures can be designed to use minimal memory while maintaining performance.

2. **Complexity vs. Performance**: Developers must strike a balance between data structure complexity and its impact on code maintainability and performance.

3. **Assembly Libraries**: In some cases, pre-built assembly libraries for data structures can be used, saving development time and ensuring correctness.

Conclusion

Advanced data structures in assembly language programming offer developers the opportunity to create memory-efficient and high-performance solutions. While implementing these data structures can be challenging, the benefits in terms of resource optimization and execution speed make them a valuable addition to an assembly programmer's toolkit.

Section 16.2: Advanced Optimization Strategies

In this section, we will explore advanced optimization strategies in assembly language programming. Optimization is a crucial aspect of assembly development, as it directly impacts the performance of your code. While writing efficient assembly code is essential, applying advanced optimization techniques can further enhance the speed and resource utilization of your programs.

Register Allocation

One of the primary optimization techniques in assembly is efficient register allocation. Registers are the fastest memory storage units available to the CPU. Efficiently using registers can significantly reduce memory access times and improve execution speed.

Example: Register Usage
```
; Inefficient register usage
mov eax, [mem1]    ; Load value from memory to eax
add ebx, eax       ; Add eax to ebx
mov ecx, [mem2]    ; Load another value from memory to ecx
sub ecx, ebx       ; Subtract ebx from ecx

; More efficient register usage
mov eax, [mem1]    ; Load value from memory to eax
mov ebx, [mem2]    ; Load another value from memory to ebx
add eax, ebx       ; Add ebx to eax
sub ecx, ebx       ; Subtract ebx from ecx
```

In the above example, the second code snippet is more efficient as it minimizes memory access and efficiently utilizes registers.

Loop Unrolling

Loop unrolling is a technique where multiple loop iterations are combined into a single iteration. This reduces loop overhead and can improve performance in certain situations. However, it increases code size.

Example: Loop Unrolling

```
; Original loop
mov ecx, 10          ; Loop counter
loop_start:
    ; Loop body
    dec ecx
    jnz loop_start

; Loop unrolled by a factor of 2
mov ecx, 5           ; Loop counter
loop_start:
    ; Loop body (iteration 1)
    ; Loop body (iteration 2)
    dec ecx
    jnz loop_start
```

Instruction Pipelining

Modern CPUs use instruction pipelines to overlap instruction fetch, decode, execution, and write-back stages. Understanding pipeline behavior is crucial for optimizing assembly code. Techniques like instruction reordering and avoiding pipeline stalls can improve performance.

Compiler Optimizations

Some assembly compilers provide optimization flags that automatically apply advanced optimization techniques. Leveraging these compiler optimizations can save development time and produce efficient code.

Profiling and Benchmarking

Profiling tools allow you to identify bottlenecks in your code, enabling you to focus your optimization efforts effectively. Benchmarking helps you compare different optimization strategies to determine which one yields the best results for your specific use case.

Conclusion

Advanced optimization strategies in assembly programming are essential for maximizing the efficiency and performance of your code. These techniques, including register allocation, loop unrolling, instruction pipelining awareness, compiler optimizations, and profiling, help you create high-performance software in the world of assembly language programming. However, it's essential to strike a balance between optimization and code readability, as overly optimized code can be challenging to maintain.

Section 16.3: Advanced Debugging Tools

In the world of assembly language programming, debugging can be challenging due to the low-level nature of the code. In this section, we'll explore advanced debugging tools and techniques that can help you diagnose and resolve issues more effectively.

Disassemblers

Disassemblers are essential tools for reverse engineering and debugging assembly code. They allow you to convert machine code back into human-readable assembly language. Some popular disassemblers include IDA Pro, OllyDbg, and radare2. These tools enable you to analyze and understand the functionality of compiled programs.

Example: Disassembly Output
```
; Original Assembly Code
mov eax, 42
add eax, ebx

; Disassembly Output
mov eax, 2Ah
add eax, ebx
```

Debugging Symbols

Debugging symbols are metadata included in the compiled binary that provide information about the source code, such as variable names, function names, and source file locations. Debuggers use these symbols to map machine code instructions to specific lines of source code.

Source-Level Debugging

Some modern debuggers, such as GDB (GNU Debugger) and WinDbg, support source-level debugging for assembly code. This means you can set breakpoints, step through code, and inspect variables at the assembly source code level, making debugging more intuitive.

Example: Source-Level Debugging in GDB
```
$ gdb my_program
(gdb) break my_function
(gdb) run
(gdb) stepi    ; Step through one assembly instruction
(gdb) info registers   ; View register values
```

Tracing and Profiling

Tracing tools like strace (for Linux) and Process Monitor (for Windows) allow you to monitor system calls and file I/O operations made by your program. Profiling tools, such as perf and gprof, help you identify performance bottlenecks by measuring CPU usage and function call frequencies.

Dynamic Analysis

Dynamic analysis tools, like Valgrind, allow you to detect memory leaks, buffer overflows, and other runtime errors in your assembly code. These tools simulate program execution and provide detailed reports on memory usage and errors.

Remote Debugging

Remote debugging tools enable you to debug assembly code running on a remote machine or device. This is especially useful for embedded systems and remote servers. GDB and LLDB support remote debugging using protocols like GDB Remote Serial Protocol (RSP).

Example: Remote Debugging with GDB

```
$ gdb
(gdb) target remote <remote_host>:<port>
(gdb) file my_program
(gdb) break main
(gdb) continue
```

Conclusion

Advanced debugging tools and techniques are indispensable for assembly language programmers. Whether you're reverse engineering, troubleshooting, or optimizing your code, these tools provide insights and visibility into the low-level operations of your programs. Familiarity with disassemblers, debugging symbols, source-level debugging, tracing, profiling, dynamic analysis, and remote debugging will make you a more effective assembly developer and help you deliver reliable and performant software.

Section 16.4: Assembly Language Patterns and Idioms

As you delve deeper into assembly language programming, you'll discover that certain coding patterns and idioms are commonly used to achieve specific tasks efficiently. These patterns represent best practices and are designed to optimize code for performance and maintainability. In this section, we'll explore some of these assembly language patterns and idioms.

Pattern 1: Looping with ecx or rcx

One of the most common patterns in assembly language is implementing loops. A loop allows you to repeat a block of code a specified number of times. In x86 assembly, the ecx register (or rcx in 64-bit mode) is often used as a loop counter.

Here's an example of a simple loop in x86 assembly:

```
section .data
    count db 10    ; Number of iterations

section .text
global main
main:
    mov ecx, 0     ; Initialize loop counter

loop_start:
    ; Your code here

    inc ecx          ; Increment the loop counter
    cmp ecx, byte [count]
    jl loop_start  ; Jump back to loop_start if ecx < count
```

Pattern 2: Procedure Call and Return

Procedures or functions are fundamental in assembly programming for modularizing code. The call instruction is used to call a procedure, and the ret instruction is used to return from it. Parameters can be passed via registers or the stack, depending on the calling convention.

```
section .text
global main
global my_function

main:
    ; Your code here
    call my_function

    ; Rest of your code
    ret

my_function:
    ; Function code here
    ret
```

Pattern 3: Memory Copy (Rep Movsb)

Copying blocks of memory is a common operation in programming. The rep movsb instruction sequence is an efficient way to perform memory copies in assembly. It repeats the movsb instruction until the specified count (in ecx) reaches zero.

```
section .data
    src db 1, 2, 3, 4, 5
    dest db 0, 0, 0, 0, 0
    count equ 5

section .text
global main
main:
    mov esi, src
    mov edi, dest
    mov ecx, count
    rep movsb
```

Pattern 4: Branching and Conditional Execution

Conditional execution is achieved using branch instructions like je (jump if equal), jne (jump if not equal), jz (jump if zero), and jnz (jump if not zero). These instructions enable you to control the flow of your program based on specific conditions.

```
section .data
    x dd 42
    y dd 24

section .text
global main
main:
    fld dword [x]
    fcom dword [y]
    fstsw ax
    sahf
    jae greater_or_equal
    ; Code to execute if x < y
    jmp done

greater_or_equal:
    ; Code to execute if x >= y

done:
    ; Rest of your code
```

Pattern 5: String Manipulation (Rep Stosb)

String manipulation, such as clearing a buffer or filling it with a specific value, is often accomplished using the rep stosb instruction sequence. It repeats the stosb instruction to store data in memory.

```
section .data
    buffer db 0, 0, 0, 0, 0
    count equ 5
    value db 42
```

```
section .text
global main
main:
    mov edi, buffer
    mov ecx, count
    mov al, value
    rep stosb
```

Conclusion

These assembly language patterns and idioms are essential for writing efficient and maintainable code. Understanding when and how to use them can significantly improve your assembly programming skills. As you gain experience, you'll develop your own set of patterns tailored to your specific applications and requirements.

Section 16.5: Case Studies in Advanced Assembly Programming

In this section, we will explore several case studies that highlight the practical application of advanced assembly programming techniques. These case studies showcase real-world scenarios where assembly language plays a crucial role in achieving specific goals. While the previous sections have provided you with a foundation in assembly programming, these case studies demonstrate how that knowledge can be applied effectively.

Case Study 1: High-Performance Multimedia Processing

Imagine you are working on a multimedia application that requires real-time video processing, such as video streaming, filtering, or transcoding. In such cases, assembly language can be employed to optimize critical sections of the code, ensuring that multimedia data is processed swiftly and efficiently. Vectorization using SIMD (Single Instruction, Multiple Data) instructions can greatly accelerate image and video processing tasks. Techniques like parallelism and multi-threading can also be utilized to maximize performance on multi-core processors.

Here's a snippet of assembly code that demonstrates the use of SIMD instructions for image convolution:

```
section .data
    src_image db ...
    dest_image db ...
    kernel db ...

section .text
global main
main:
    movaps xmm0, [kernel]
    mov esi, src_image
```

```
    mov edi, dest_image
    xorps xmm1, xmm1    ; Clear xmm1 register

process_pixel:
    movdqu xmm2, [esi]  ; Load 16 bytes (4 pixels) from source
    pmaddubsw xmm2, xmm0  ; Multiply and accumulate
    paddw xmm1, xmm2    ; Add to accumulated result
    movdqu [edi], xmm1  ; Store result
    add esi, 16
    add edi, 16
    cmp esi, end_of_image
    jl process_pixel
```

Case Study 2: Real-Time Game Engine

Developing a high-performance game engine often involves writing critical components in assembly language. Graphics rendering, physics simulations, and collision detection are examples of tasks where assembly optimization can significantly boost frame rates and overall game performance. Assembly allows you to work closely with the hardware, taking full advantage of the GPU and CPU capabilities.

Here's a simplified example of an assembly routine for 2D collision detection in a game:

```
section .data
    player_rect db 10, 10, 30, 30   ; Player's bounding box
    obstacle_rect db 20, 20, 40, 40   ; Obstacle's bounding box

section .text
global main
main:
    ; Load player_rect and obstacle_rect
    ; Calculate collision detection
    ; Set flags or take action based on collision
```

Case Study 3: Cryptography and Secure Systems

Security-critical applications often rely on assembly language to implement cryptographic algorithms efficiently. Cryptography demands precise control over data manipulation and protection against various attacks. Assembly allows for fine-grained control and optimization of cryptographic operations, ensuring the confidentiality and integrity of sensitive information.

Here's a simplified example of assembly code implementing the AES encryption algorithm:

```
section .data
    plaintext db ...
    key db ...

section .text
global main
```

```
main:
    ; Load plaintext and encryption key
    ; Perform AES encryption
    ; Store the encrypted result
```

Case Study 4: Embedded Systems and IoT

Embedded systems and IoT devices frequently utilize assembly language to meet stringent resource constraints, optimize power consumption, and achieve real-time performance. Assembly code for embedded systems is often tailored to specific hardware platforms, ensuring efficient utilization of limited resources.

Here's a snippet of assembly code for a simple IoT device that controls an LED based on sensor input:

```
section .data
    sensor_value dd 0
    threshold dd 100

section .text
global main
main:
    ; Read sensor value
    ; Compare with threshold
    ; Control LED based on the comparison
```

These case studies illustrate the versatility and power of assembly language in various domains, from multimedia processing and game development to cryptography and embedded systems. While assembly programming may be challenging, mastering it opens doors to optimizing software for performance-critical applications.

Chapter 17: Assembly Language for AI and Machine Learning

Section 17.1: Introduction to AI and ML

In recent years, Artificial Intelligence (AI) and Machine Learning (ML) have gained significant prominence in various industries, revolutionizing the way we solve complex problems and make data-driven decisions. These fields have witnessed remarkable growth, with applications spanning from natural language processing and computer vision to autonomous vehicles and healthcare diagnostics. In this section, we will introduce the fundamental concepts of AI and ML and explore how assembly language can be leveraged in this domain.

Understanding AI and ML

AI refers to the simulation of human intelligence in machines that are programmed to think and learn like humans. ML, a subset of AI, focuses on the development of algorithms that enable computers to learn from and make predictions or decisions based on data. ML models can identify patterns, make recommendations, and improve their performance over time through continuous learning.

AI and ML in Assembly

While AI and ML applications are typically developed in high-level programming languages like Python or R due to their extensive libraries and frameworks, assembly language can play a crucial role in certain aspects of AI and ML implementation, particularly when performance optimization is essential.

1. **Accelerating AI Models**: Assembly language can be used to optimize critical sections of AI and ML algorithms, such as matrix multiplication in neural networks. SIMD (Single Instruction, Multiple Data) instructions and parallelization techniques can significantly speed up these computations.

2. **Interface with Hardware**: Assembly is often employed to interface with specialized hardware accelerators like GPUs (Graphics Processing Units) or TPUs (Tensor Processing Units), which are commonly used in AI and ML workloads.

3. **Real-Time Applications**: In scenarios where real-time processing is critical, such as autonomous vehicles or robotics, assembly language can ensure that AI and ML models run with minimal latency, meeting stringent response time requirements.

4. **Security**: Security is paramount in AI and ML applications, especially in areas like cybersecurity and fraud detection. Assembly language allows for precise control over data encryption, decryption, and secure key management.

Here's a simplified example of how assembly language can be used to optimize the matrix multiplication operation, a fundamental operation in many ML algorithms:

```
section .data
    matrix_A dd ...
    matrix_B dd ...
    result_matrix dd ...

section .text
global main
main:
    ; Load matrices A and B
    ; Perform matrix multiplication using SIMD instructions
    ; Store the result in the result_matrix
```

In this example, assembly code takes advantage of SIMD instructions to accelerate matrix multiplication, improving the performance of AI and ML models that rely on this operation.

As we delve deeper into this chapter, we will explore more advanced topics, including implementing neural networks in assembly, conducting machine learning inference efficiently, and applying AI and ML techniques in robotics. Assembly language, when used judiciously, can enhance the capabilities and performance of AI and ML systems in a variety of contexts.

Section 17.2: Implementing Neural Networks in Assembly

Neural networks are the backbone of many AI and machine learning applications, ranging from image recognition to natural language processing. These networks consist of layers of interconnected nodes (neurons) that process and transform input data to produce meaningful outputs. Implementing neural networks efficiently is crucial for AI and ML tasks, and in some cases, assembly language can be used to optimize critical parts of neural network operations.

Challenges of Neural Network Implementation in Assembly

Implementing neural networks in assembly language poses several challenges due to the complexity of these models:

1. **Algorithm Complexity**: Neural networks involve a multitude of mathematical operations, including matrix multiplications, element-wise operations, and nonlinear activations. Writing and optimizing these operations in assembly can be intricate and error-prone.

2. **Portability**: Assembly code is platform-specific and may not be easily portable to different hardware architectures or operating systems. This limits the reusability of assembly-based neural network implementations.

3. **Debugging and Maintenance**: Assembly code is known for being challenging to debug and maintain, making it less desirable for complex projects like neural networks where code changes and updates are frequent.

Despite these challenges, assembly language can still play a valuable role in neural network implementation, especially for performance-critical components.

SIMD Instructions for Neural Networks

One area where assembly shines in neural network implementation is the utilization of SIMD (Single Instruction, Multiple Data) instructions available in modern CPUs. SIMD instructions enable parallel processing of data elements, making them well-suited for tasks like element-wise operations and matrix multiplications commonly found in neural networks.

Here's a simplified example of how SIMD instructions can be used in assembly to accelerate a common neural network operation, the ReLU (Rectified Linear Unit) activation function:

```
section .data
    input_data dd ...
    output_data dd ...

section .text
global relu
relu:
    movaps   xmm0, [rdi]    ; Load input_data into xmm0
    xorps    xmm1, xmm1     ; Clear xmm1 (xmm1 = 0)
    maxps    xmm0, xmm1     ; Apply ReLU function element-wise
    movaps   [rsi], xmm0    ; Store the result in output_data
    ret
```

In this assembly code, the maxps instruction is used to perform element-wise ReLU activation efficiently on a vector of data. This type of operation can be part of a larger neural network implementation, where SIMD instructions help improve performance.

Beyond Low-Level Optimization

While assembly language can be used for low-level optimization of neural networks, it's worth noting that high-level libraries and frameworks like TensorFlow and PyTorch provide extensive support for neural network development, abstracting many low-level details. These frameworks often use highly optimized CPU and GPU implementations under the hood, making them the preferred choice for most neural network projects.

In this chapter, we will explore how assembly language can complement high-level neural network frameworks and be used when specific optimizations are needed. We'll also discuss techniques for interfacing assembly code with neural network libraries, allowing you to harness the power of assembly where it matters most.

Section 17.3: Machine Learning Inference in Assembly

Machine learning inference, the process of using a trained model to make predictions on new data, is a critical aspect of AI and ML applications. While high-level frameworks like TensorFlow and PyTorch dominate the landscape for model training and deployment, there are scenarios where optimizing the inference process using assembly language can offer significant advantages.

The Need for Inference Optimization

Inference tasks often involve running models on resource-constrained devices, such as edge devices, IoT sensors, and mobile devices. These devices may have limited computational power, memory, or battery life. In such cases, optimizing the inference process becomes crucial to meet performance and efficiency requirements.

Assembly language can be leveraged to optimize specific parts of the inference pipeline, especially when working with hardware accelerators like CPUs and GPUs that support SIMD (Single Instruction, Multiple Data) operations. Optimizations at this level can lead to faster inference times and reduced power consumption.

Optimizing Matrix Operations

One of the key areas where assembly language shines in machine learning inference is optimizing matrix operations, which are fundamental to many neural network models. Libraries like BLAS (Basic Linear Algebra Subprograms) provide highly optimized matrix operations, but fine-tuning these operations further in assembly can provide performance benefits.

Here's a simplified example of matrix multiplication in assembly:

```
section .data
    matrix_A dd ...
    matrix_B dd ...
    result_matrix dd ...

section .text
global matrix_multiply
matrix_multiply:
    ; Load matrix_A, matrix_B, and dimensions into registers
    ...

    ; Perform matrix multiplication
    ...

    ; Store the result in result_matrix
    ...
```

```
ret
```

In this assembly code, we load two matrices, perform matrix multiplication, and store the result. By optimizing the matrix multiplication algorithm at the assembly level, we can achieve faster inference times, which is crucial for real-time applications.

Custom Hardware Acceleration

In some cases, especially when working with specialized hardware like FPGAs (Field-Programmable Gate Arrays) or custom accelerators, writing assembly code may be the only way to fully leverage the capabilities of the hardware. This level of control allows developers to implement custom inference pipelines tailored to the specific hardware architecture.

However, it's essential to strike a balance between using assembly language for low-level optimization and leveraging high-level libraries and frameworks for model loading, preprocessing, and postprocessing. This hybrid approach ensures that you can harness the full power of assembly where it's most beneficial while maintaining code maintainability and portability.

Conclusion

Machine learning inference in assembly language is a specialized area that requires a deep understanding of both machine learning algorithms and assembly programming. While it may not be the default choice for most ML projects, it offers a unique advantage in scenarios where performance optimization is critical, and hardware constraints demand low-level control. In this section, we've explored the need for inference optimization, highlighted areas where assembly can excel, and discussed the balance between low-level and high-level approaches in machine learning inference.

Section 17.4: AI-Driven Robotics

AI-driven robotics represents a fascinating intersection of artificial intelligence and robotics, where advanced algorithms enable robots to perceive and interact with the world intelligently. In this section, we'll explore the role of assembly language in AI-driven robotics and how it contributes to the development of intelligent robotic systems.

The Marriage of AI and Robotics

Artificial intelligence has revolutionized robotics by providing robots with the ability to sense, think, and act autonomously. Machine learning techniques, such as computer vision, natural language processing, and reinforcement learning, empower robots to understand their environment, make decisions, and adapt to changing situations.

Assembly language plays a crucial role in this synergy by optimizing the low-level control and coordination of robotic hardware. Robots often require real-time responsiveness and precise control over motors, sensors, and actuators. Assembly is well-suited for these tasks due to its efficiency and deterministic execution.

Low-Level Control and Sensor Integration

One of the primary applications of assembly language in AI-driven robotics is low-level control. Robots rely on sensors to gather data about their surroundings, including cameras, lidar, accelerometers, and gyroscopes. Assembly code is used to interface with these sensors, process data, and make rapid decisions based on sensor inputs.

For example, in a self-driving car, assembly language may be employed to process camera images for object detection or lidar data for mapping and localization. These critical tasks demand the utmost efficiency to ensure real-time response and safety.

Motor Control and Actuation

Efficient motor control is another area where assembly shines. Robots use various types of motors and actuators to move and manipulate objects. Assembly code can be tailored to control these motors precisely, enabling robots to perform tasks with accuracy and speed.

In industrial automation, assembly language is often used to control robotic arms for tasks like welding, painting, or pick-and-place operations. The ability to control motors at the assembly level ensures that robots can carry out tasks with submillimeter precision.

Real-Time Decision Making

Assembly language is also employed for real-time decision making in robotics. When robots need to react quickly to changing conditions, such as avoiding obstacles or responding to user commands, assembly code can handle these tasks with minimal latency.

Consider a drone that uses assembly language to process sensor data and adjust its flight path in real-time to avoid collisions. In such applications, assembly is invaluable for ensuring rapid response and safety.

Conclusion

AI-driven robotics is a burgeoning field that promises to reshape industries ranging from healthcare and manufacturing to transportation and agriculture. Assembly language's role in this domain is to provide the low-level control and efficiency necessary for robots to interact with the physical world intelligently.

While high-level programming languages and AI frameworks are used for algorithm development and higher-level control, assembly remains a vital tool for optimizing robotic hardware and ensuring real-time responsiveness. The marriage of AI and assembly empowers robots to perform complex tasks with precision and efficiency, opening up a world of possibilities for intelligent automation.

Section 17.5: AI and ML Applications in Assembly

Artificial Intelligence (AI) and Machine Learning (ML) have become integral parts of numerous applications across various domains. In this section, we'll explore how assembly language can be leveraged for AI and ML applications, showcasing the unique capabilities it offers in this context.

Optimizing AI and ML Algorithms

AI and ML algorithms often involve complex mathematical computations, such as matrix multiplications, convolutions, and statistical operations. These algorithms can be computationally intensive, especially when processing large datasets. Assembly language, known for its efficiency and low-level control over hardware resources, can be employed to optimize critical sections of AI and ML code.

For instance, in deep learning frameworks like TensorFlow or PyTorch, assembly language routines can accelerate the computation of neural network layers. By directly utilizing hardware features like SIMD (Single Instruction, Multiple Data) instructions, assembly code can significantly speed up matrix operations, leading to faster training and inference times.

Hardware-Specific Optimization

Different hardware architectures, such as CPUs, GPUs, and accelerators like TPUs (Tensor Processing Units), have unique features and instruction sets. Assembly language enables developers to write platform-specific code that takes full advantage of the available hardware capabilities.

In AI and ML, this means optimizing algorithms for the target hardware to achieve maximum performance. Assembly can be utilized to exploit GPU parallelism, access specialized AI hardware instructions, and implement custom kernels tailored to the hardware architecture.

Real-Time AI Applications

Some AI applications require real-time processing, such as autonomous vehicles, robotics, and industrial automation. Assembly language's deterministic execution and low-latency characteristics make it an excellent choice for implementing real-time AI components.

Consider a self-driving car that needs to process sensor data and make split-second decisions. Assembly code can efficiently handle tasks like object detection, lane tracking, and collision avoidance, ensuring rapid responses to changing road conditions.

Hardware Abstraction

Assembly language provides a high degree of control over hardware resources, allowing developers to fine-tune AI and ML applications for specific hardware configurations. It serves as a bridge between high-level AI frameworks and the underlying hardware.

Moreover, assembly language can be used to write hardware abstraction layers (HALs) that facilitate AI and ML application development across different hardware platforms. This enables developers to write code that is more portable and adaptable to various computing environments.

Conclusion

AI and ML are at the forefront of technological advancements, driving innovation in fields such as healthcare, finance, natural language processing, computer vision, and more. Assembly language, with its efficiency, low-level control, and hardware optimization capabilities, plays a crucial role in accelerating AI and ML applications.

While high-level languages and AI frameworks provide productivity and ease of development, assembly language remains a valuable tool for fine-tuning critical sections of code, optimizing for specific hardware, and achieving real-time performance in AI-driven systems. As AI continues to transform industries, assembly's role in hardware-level optimization and real-time processing will remain relevant in the pursuit of AI-driven innovations.

Chapter 18: Assembly Language for Quantum Computing

Section 18.1: Quantum Computing Basics

Quantum computing represents a paradigm shift in computational power and capability. In this section, we'll delve into the fundamental concepts of quantum computing and explore how assembly language can be applied to harness the potential of this revolutionary technology.

Understanding Quantum Bits (Qubits)

At the heart of quantum computing are qubits, which are the quantum analogs of classical bits. Unlike classical bits, which can only exist in a state of 0 or 1, qubits can exist in multiple states simultaneously due to the principles of superposition. This property allows quantum computers to perform certain calculations exponentially faster than classical computers.

Qubits can be implemented using various physical systems, such as trapped ions, superconducting circuits, and photons. Assembly language can be used to program the control and manipulation of these physical qubits.

Quantum Gates and Operations

Quantum computation involves the use of quantum gates to manipulate qubits. These gates perform operations that can entangle qubits, create superpositions, and perform quantum Fourier transforms, among other things. Assembly code can be written to control the timing and sequence of quantum gates in a quantum processor.

Understanding the assembly-level control of quantum gates is crucial for optimizing quantum algorithms. This level of control allows developers to implement custom error-correction codes, which are vital for maintaining the integrity of quantum computations.

Quantum Algorithms in Assembly

Assembly language can be employed to implement quantum algorithms efficiently. Prominent algorithms like Shor's algorithm for integer factorization and Grover's algorithm for searching unsorted databases can benefit from fine-grained control over quantum gates and qubit states.

Developing quantum algorithms in assembly requires a deep understanding of quantum mechanics and the hardware architecture of quantum processors. Additionally, quantum programming languages like QASM (Quantum Assembly Language) provide a bridge between high-level quantum algorithms and low-level assembly code.

Challenges and Opportunities

Quantum computing is still in its nascent stages, and there are numerous technical challenges to overcome. These challenges include qubit stability, error correction, and scaling quantum systems to handle practical problems. Assembly language plays a crucial role in addressing these challenges by providing the low-level control needed for optimization and error management.

Quantum assembly programming requires a unique skill set that combines quantum physics, computer architecture, and assembly language expertise. As quantum hardware evolves and becomes more accessible, mastering quantum assembly programming will be essential for quantum software development.

Conclusion

Quantum computing has the potential to revolutionize fields ranging from cryptography to materials science and drug discovery. Assembly language, with its ability to provide precise control over quantum hardware, is poised to be a critical tool in unlocking the full potential of quantum computing. While quantum assembly programming is still in its infancy, it offers a fascinating and promising frontier for software developers and scientists alike.

Section 18.2: Quantum Algorithms in Assembly

In the world of quantum computing, developing and implementing quantum algorithms is a significant area of interest. Quantum algorithms are designed to harness the unique properties of qubits, such as superposition and entanglement, to solve problems more efficiently than classical algorithms. In this section, we will explore how quantum algorithms can be expressed and executed using assembly language.

Expressing Quantum Algorithms

Quantum algorithms are typically expressed using a specialized quantum programming language or framework. One of the most well-known quantum programming languages is Qiskit, developed by IBM. Qiskit allows developers to design quantum circuits and algorithms at a high level. However, to achieve fine-grained control and optimization, quantum programmers often turn to assembly-like representations.

Assembly-level quantum programming involves specifying quantum gates and their sequences directly. These gates are analogous to the logic gates used in classical computing but operate on qubits in quantum superposition. For example, the Hadamard gate is frequently used to create superpositions, while controlled-NOT (CNOT) gates enable entanglement.

Advantages of Quantum Assembly

Quantum assembly language provides several advantages when working with quantum algorithms:

1. **Fine-Grained Control:** With quantum assembly, developers have precise control over the execution of quantum gates. This level of control is essential for optimizing quantum algorithms for specific quantum hardware.

2. **Customization:** Quantum assembly allows for the customization of error-correction codes and fault-tolerant quantum circuits. This is crucial for mitigating errors in quantum computations.

3. **Quantum Hardware Compatibility:** Quantum assembly code can be tailored to specific quantum hardware architectures, ensuring efficient use of available qubits and minimizing gate errors.

Quantum Algorithm Examples

Let's briefly explore two famous quantum algorithms and how they can be expressed in quantum assembly:

1. Shor's Algorithm

Shor's algorithm is a quantum algorithm that efficiently factors large integers, a task that is classically very time-consuming. In quantum assembly, the algorithm involves a series of quantum gates that apply modular arithmetic operations and Fourier transforms to find the factors of a number.

```
# Quantum assembly code for Shor's algorithm (simplified)
initialize qubits
apply Hadamard gates
apply quantum Fourier transform
measure qubits
apply classical post-processing
```

2. Grover's Algorithm

Grover's algorithm is used for unstructured search and can provide a quadratic speedup compared to classical search algorithms. Quantum assembly code for Grover's algorithm involves applying a series of Grover operators iteratively.

```
# Quantum assembly code for Grover's algorithm (simplified)
initialize qubits
apply Grover operators iteratively
measure qubits and perform amplitude amplification
```

Challenges and Future Directions

Quantum assembly programming is a specialized skill that requires a deep understanding of both quantum mechanics and quantum hardware. As quantum technologies continue to evolve, quantum assembly languages and frameworks are likely to become more sophisticated and user-friendly.

In the coming years, we can expect the development of new quantum algorithms and optimization techniques, and quantum assembly will play a vital role in implementing and fine-tuning these algorithms for practical applications. As quantum computers become more accessible, mastering quantum assembly will be a valuable skill for researchers and developers in the quantum computing field.

Section 18.3: Quantum Simulators and Hardware

In the realm of quantum computing, the availability of quantum simulators and quantum hardware is crucial for the development and testing of quantum algorithms. In this section, we will explore the role of quantum simulators and the state of quantum hardware, including quantum processors.

Quantum Simulators

Quantum simulators are software tools designed to mimic the behavior of quantum computers without using actual quantum hardware. They are essential for quantum algorithm development and testing because they allow researchers and developers to experiment with quantum algorithms and circuits in a controlled environment.

Types of Quantum Simulators
1. **State Vector Simulators:** These simulators keep track of the quantum state of the system using a state vector. They are suitable for small quantum systems but become impractical for larger systems due to exponential memory requirements.

2. **Density Matrix Simulators:** Density matrix simulators can handle mixed quantum states and are more memory-efficient for simulating larger quantum systems. They are commonly used for noisy quantum circuits.

3. **Gate-Based Simulators:** Gate-based simulators simulate quantum gates' operations and are used to estimate the quantum circuit's behavior. They are efficient for simulating noisy intermediate-scale quantum (NISQ) circuits.

Quantum Simulator Usage

Quantum simulators are widely used for various purposes:

- **Algorithm Development:** Researchers use simulators to develop and test quantum algorithms before running them on actual quantum hardware. Simulators provide a safe environment to work out algorithmic details and debug code.

- **Error Mitigation:** Simulators help study and mitigate noise and errors that occur in quantum hardware. By simulating noisy conditions, researchers can develop error-correction techniques.

- **Educational Tools:** Quantum simulators serve as valuable educational tools for teaching quantum computing concepts. They allow students to experiment with quantum algorithms without access to physical quantum devices.

Quantum Hardware

Quantum hardware refers to physical quantum processors that execute quantum algorithms. Quantum processors are the heart of quantum computers and come in various forms, including superconducting qubit-based processors, trapped-ion processors, and others.

Superconducting Qubits

Superconducting qubits are among the most widely used quantum bits in quantum processors. These qubits operate at extremely low temperatures and exhibit longer coherence times, making them suitable for implementing quantum algorithms. Companies like IBM, Google, and Rigetti have developed superconducting qubit-based quantum processors.

Trapped-Ion Qubits

Trapped-ion qubits are another promising technology for quantum processors. They use ions (charged atoms) trapped in electromagnetic fields to represent quantum bits. Companies like IonQ have developed trapped-ion quantum processors.

Challenges in Quantum Hardware

While quantum hardware holds great promise, there are significant challenges:

- **Quantum Error Correction:** Quantum processors are inherently noisy. Developing robust quantum error correction codes is essential to make quantum computations reliable.

- **Scalability:** Building larger and more powerful quantum processors is a substantial engineering challenge. Scalability is a key focus for quantum hardware developers.

- **Cryogenic Cooling:** Many quantum processors require cryogenic cooling, which adds to their complexity and cost.

Hybrid Quantum Computing

Hybrid quantum computing combines classical and quantum computation to address real-world problems. In hybrid approaches, quantum processors are used to accelerate specific tasks within classical algorithms. This approach is especially relevant as quantum hardware becomes more accessible and powerful.

In conclusion, quantum simulators play a crucial role in quantum algorithm development and error mitigation. Quantum hardware, including superconducting and trapped-ion qubits, is advancing rapidly but faces challenges related to noise and scalability. As quantum computing matures, the synergy between simulators and hardware will continue to drive progress in this exciting field.

Section 18.4: Quantum Cryptography

Quantum cryptography represents a paradigm shift in secure communication. Unlike classical cryptographic methods that rely on computational complexity, quantum cryptography leverages the fundamental principles of quantum mechanics to ensure the security of communication channels. In this section, we delve into the principles and applications of quantum cryptography.

Quantum Key Distribution (QKD)

Quantum Key Distribution (QKD) is a cornerstone of quantum cryptography. It enables two parties, traditionally referred to as Alice and Bob, to establish a secret key with unconditional security. The security of QKD relies on the fundamental properties of quantum mechanics:

- **Superposition:** A quantum bit, or qubit, can exist in multiple states simultaneously, allowing Alice to prepare qubits in various states.

- **Entanglement:** Qubits can be entangled, meaning that the state of one qubit is dependent on the state of another, even when they are separated by long distances.

- **Quantum Uncertainty:** The act of measuring a qubit inherently disturbs its state, which can be detected by the parties involved.

QKD protocols, such as the BB84 protocol, exploit these properties to establish a shared secret key between Alice and Bob. The key is generated using qubits, and any eavesdropping attempt by an adversary, often referred to as Eve, can be detected due to the disturbance caused by quantum measurements.

Quantum Secure Communication

Beyond key distribution, quantum cryptography offers secure communication methods that leverage quantum principles:

- **Quantum Teleportation:** Quantum teleportation allows the transfer of a qubit's quantum state from one location to another, without physically moving the qubit. This can be used to transmit quantum keys securely.

- **Quantum Encryption:** Quantum encryption algorithms, such as Quantum Key Distribution-based encryption, use shared quantum keys to encrypt and decrypt messages. This ensures that the communication is secure from eavesdropping attempts.

- **Quantum-Safe Algorithms:** Quantum computers, once they reach a sufficient scale, may break classical encryption methods, posing a security risk. Quantum-safe algorithms, designed to resist quantum attacks, are being developed to secure classical communication in a post-quantum era.

Quantum Cryptography Challenges

While quantum cryptography offers exciting possibilities, it faces several practical challenges:

- **Distance Limitations:** Quantum entanglement and qubit transmission are limited by the distance between the communicating parties. Current technologies are suitable for secure communication over relatively short distances.

- **Hardware Development:** Building reliable and practical quantum cryptography hardware, including quantum repeaters, is a significant engineering challenge.

- **Cost:** Quantum cryptography hardware can be expensive, limiting its widespread adoption.

- **Real-World Deployment:** Integrating quantum cryptography into existing communication infrastructure requires careful planning and investment.

Quantum Cryptography Applications

Quantum cryptography has several promising applications:

- **Secure Communications:** Quantum cryptography can ensure the confidentiality and integrity of communications between parties, even in the presence of powerful adversaries.

- **Financial Transactions:** Secure financial transactions, such as online banking and cryptocurrency transfers, can benefit from quantum cryptography to protect against quantum attacks.

- **Government and Defense:** Governments and defense organizations can use quantum cryptography for secure communication and data protection.

- **Healthcare and Medical Research:** Secure transmission of medical data and research findings is crucial, making quantum cryptography valuable in healthcare and scientific research.

In summary, quantum cryptography offers a new era of secure communication by harnessing the principles of quantum mechanics. While facing practical challenges, it holds great potential for revolutionizing the way we ensure the confidentiality and integrity of sensitive information in various domains.

Section 18.5: Quantum Assembly Programming Challenges

Quantum computing is an emerging field with the potential to revolutionize computational capabilities. As quantum hardware becomes more accessible and powerful, there is a growing interest in programming at the quantum level. In this section, we explore the challenges associated with quantum assembly programming.

Quantum Hardware Variability

One of the primary challenges in quantum assembly programming is the inherent variability of quantum hardware. Unlike classical computers, where bits are deterministic, quantum bits or qubits are probabilistic due to the principles of quantum mechanics. This variability introduces uncertainty in program execution, making it challenging to write reliable and predictable quantum assembly code.

Programmers must account for errors introduced by factors such as qubit decoherence, gate imperfections, and environmental noise. Developing error-correcting codes and techniques for fault tolerance is a critical aspect of quantum assembly programming.

Quantum Parallelism

Quantum computers leverage quantum parallelism to perform certain tasks exponentially faster than classical computers. While this is a significant advantage, it also presents challenges. Quantum assembly programmers must harness this parallelism effectively, which often requires a different mindset compared to classical programming.

Optimizing quantum algorithms for specific hardware architectures is a complex task. This involves mapping quantum circuits to physical qubits, minimizing gate count, and optimizing for quantum parallelism.

Quantum Algorithm Design

Quantum assembly programmers face the task of designing and implementing quantum algorithms. This process involves translating complex mathematical algorithms into quantum circuits composed of gates and qubits. Quantum algorithm design requires a deep understanding of quantum mechanics and mathematical concepts.

Additionally, developing quantum algorithms often involves solving problems with no known classical solutions. This requires creativity and innovation in algorithm design.

Quantum Programming Languages

Quantum assembly programming often interfaces with higher-level quantum programming languages, such as Q# or Quipper, which provide abstractions for quantum circuit creation. However, these languages are still evolving, and their compilers may not fully optimize code for specific quantum hardware.

Programmers must bridge the gap between quantum assembly and higher-level languages, making decisions about which parts of the code should be written in each language to achieve the best performance and maintainability.

Quantum Debugging and Testing

Debugging quantum assembly code presents unique challenges. Traditional debugging techniques are not directly applicable due to the probabilistic and non-deterministic nature of quantum computation. Quantum debugging tools are still in their infancy, making it challenging to identify and resolve errors effectively.

Testing quantum algorithms is also complex. Verifying the correctness of a quantum algorithm often requires extensive simulation, which can be computationally expensive.

Quantum Compilation and Optimization

Compiling quantum assembly code to run on physical hardware is a complex task. Quantum compilers must consider hardware constraints, qubit connectivity, gate error rates, and optimization for quantum parallelism. Writing efficient quantum assembly code that can be effectively compiled to target hardware is a non-trivial endeavor.

Quantum Hardware Access

Access to quantum hardware is currently limited and often requires collaboration with quantum computing companies or research institutions. This access challenge can hinder the development and testing of quantum assembly programs.

In conclusion, quantum assembly programming presents unique challenges related to hardware variability, quantum parallelism, algorithm design, programming languages, debugging, testing, compilation, and hardware access. Overcoming these challenges is crucial for realizing the full potential of quantum computing and its applications in various domains, including cryptography, optimization, and materials science. As quantum hardware continues to advance, quantum assembly programming will play a pivotal role in shaping the future of quantum computing.

Chapter 19: Ethical and Legal Aspects of Assembly Programming

Section 19.1: Intellectual Property and Copyright

Intellectual property (IP) and copyright laws are essential considerations in the realm of assembly programming, as they govern the use, distribution, and modification of software and related materials. In this section, we will delve into the key aspects of intellectual property and copyright relevant to assembly programming.

Intellectual property refers to the legal rights that creators have over their intellectual creations. These creations can include inventions, literary and artistic works, designs, symbols, names, and images. In the context of assembly programming, intellectual property primarily pertains to software and associated code.

Copyright Protection

Copyright is a form of intellectual property protection that grants the creator of an original work exclusive rights to its use and distribution. In many countries, copyright protection is automatically granted upon the creation of an original work, including software. This means that as soon as you write code in assembly or any other programming language, you automatically hold copyright over that code.

Open Source and Licensing

While copyright provides automatic protection, programmers often choose to release their code under open-source licenses. Open-source licenses allow others to use, modify, and distribute the code under certain conditions specified in the license. It is essential to understand the terms of the license under which you receive or use assembly code, as these terms can vary widely.

Ethical Considerations

Ethical considerations play a significant role in assembly programming. When using or distributing assembly code, it is essential to respect the intellectual property rights of the original creators. This includes adhering to the terms of open-source licenses, providing proper attribution, and not using code for unethical or malicious purposes.

Avoiding Plagiarism

Plagiarism, the act of using someone else's work without proper attribution or permission, is unethical and, in many cases, illegal. When incorporating assembly code from external sources into your projects, it is crucial to give credit to the original authors and ensure that you have the right to use the code according to its licensing terms.

Protecting Your Work

If you are the creator of assembly code, you can take steps to protect your intellectual property rights. This includes clearly specifying the licensing terms under which your code can be used and enforcing those terms if they are violated. It is also advisable to keep records of your work and any licensing agreements.

Legal Implications

Violating copyright or intellectual property rights in the context of assembly programming can have legal consequences. Legal actions can be taken against individuals or organizations that infringe on these rights. Therefore, it is essential to be aware of the laws and regulations in your jurisdiction related to intellectual property and copyright.

Conclusion

In the world of assembly programming, understanding and respecting intellectual property and copyright laws is fundamental. Whether you are a code creator or user, it is crucial to be aware of the legal and ethical aspects surrounding software development and distribution. By doing so, you can ensure that your work complies with the applicable laws and regulations and contribute positively to the assembly programming community.

Section 19.2: Responsible Hacking and Vulnerability Disclosure

Responsible hacking and vulnerability disclosure are essential practices in the field of assembly programming and cybersecurity. In this section, we will explore the principles of responsible hacking, the importance of identifying and disclosing vulnerabilities, and the role of ethical hackers in enhancing system security.

Responsible Hacking

Responsible hacking, often referred to as ethical hacking or white-hat hacking, involves probing computer systems and software for vulnerabilities with the permission of the system owner. The goal is to identify and address security weaknesses before malicious hackers can exploit them. Responsible hackers use their skills to protect and improve the security of systems rather than to harm or exploit them.

The Role of Ethical Hackers

Ethical hackers play a crucial role in helping organizations identify and address security vulnerabilities. They use their expertise to simulate real-world cyberattacks and assess the security posture of systems, networks, and software applications. This proactive approach to security helps organizations strengthen their defenses and protect sensitive data.

Vulnerability Disclosure

When ethical hackers discover vulnerabilities, responsible disclosure is essential. Vulnerability disclosure involves notifying the affected organization or software developer about the identified security issue. This allows the organization to take appropriate measures to patch or mitigate the vulnerability before it can be exploited by malicious actors.

Coordinated Disclosure

Coordinated disclosure is a structured approach to vulnerability reporting. Ethical hackers work closely with the affected organization to ensure that the vulnerability is addressed responsibly. This often involves establishing a timeline for disclosure, verifying the vulnerability, and collaborating on a fix.

Many organizations encourage responsible hacking by offering bug bounty programs. These programs reward ethical hackers for identifying and responsibly disclosing security vulnerabilities. Bug bounty programs provide an incentive for security researchers to uncover and report issues while helping organizations improve their security.

Legal Protections

In many jurisdictions, ethical hackers are protected by laws and regulations that shield them from legal liability when conducting security research with permission. However, it is essential to adhere to the terms and conditions set by the organization and act within the boundaries of the law.

Responsible Hacking Tools

Responsible hackers often use a variety of tools and techniques to identify vulnerabilities. These tools may include network scanners, vulnerability scanners, and penetration testing frameworks. However, it is crucial to use these tools responsibly and only on systems for which you have explicit permission.

Conclusion

Responsible hacking and vulnerability disclosure are integral to maintaining a secure digital environment. Ethical hackers play a vital role in helping organizations identify and remediate vulnerabilities, ultimately strengthening the cybersecurity landscape. By adhering to ethical standards and working collaboratively with organizations, responsible hackers contribute to a safer online world for all users.

Section 19.3: Ethical Considerations in Reverse Engineering

Reverse engineering is a crucial activity in various domains, including software development, hardware design, and cybersecurity. In this section, we will delve into the ethical considerations that should guide reverse engineers to ensure responsible and lawful practices.

Understanding Reverse Engineering

Reverse engineering involves analyzing and deconstructing a product or system to understand its design, functionality, or vulnerabilities. While reverse engineering can provide valuable insights, it must be conducted ethically and within the bounds of the law.

Ethical Guidelines for Reverse Engineering

1. **Obtain Legal Consent:** Before engaging in reverse engineering, ensure that you have the legal right or explicit permission to do so. Unauthorized reverse engineering can lead to legal consequences.

2. **Protect Intellectual Property:** Respect intellectual property rights, including patents, copyrights, and trade secrets. Reverse engineering should not involve stealing or misappropriating proprietary information.

3. **Non-Destructive Analysis:** Whenever possible, perform reverse engineering in a non-destructive manner, preserving the integrity of the original product or system.

4. **Use of Publicly Available Information:** Rely on publicly available information and documentation for reverse engineering. Avoid using proprietary or confidential data obtained through unethical means.

5. **Reverse Engineering for Compatibility:** Reverse engineering for the purpose of achieving compatibility with other systems or software is often considered a legitimate and ethical practice, provided it complies with legal requirements.

6. **Responsible Disclosure:** If reverse engineering reveals security vulnerabilities or flaws, follow responsible disclosure practices. Notify the affected parties and collaborate on solutions rather than exploiting the vulnerabilities for malicious purposes.

7. **Educational and Research Purposes:** Reverse engineering for educational or research purposes is generally acceptable, provided it adheres to ethical standards and legal requirements.

8. **Adherence to Ethical Codes:** Many professional organizations and associations have ethical codes and guidelines for reverse engineering. Adhere to these standards to ensure responsible conduct.

Legal Considerations

Legal frameworks related to reverse engineering can vary by jurisdiction and context. It's essential to be aware of and comply with relevant laws and regulations when conducting reverse engineering activities. Laws such as the Digital Millennium Copyright Act (DMCA) in the United States include provisions related to reverse engineering and anti-circumvention.

Conclusion

Reverse engineering is a valuable practice that can lead to innovation, improved compatibility, and enhanced cybersecurity. However, it must be approached with ethics and legality in mind. By following ethical guidelines and respecting intellectual property rights, reverse engineers can contribute positively to their respective fields while avoiding legal pitfalls.

Section 19.4: Legal Implications of Malware Analysis

Malware analysis is a critical cybersecurity practice aimed at understanding the behavior, functionality, and impact of malicious software. In this section, we will explore the legal considerations and implications that researchers and analysts should be aware of when conducting malware analysis.

Understanding Malware Analysis

Malware analysis involves dissecting and studying malicious software, such as viruses, worms, Trojans, and ransomware. The goals of malware analysis include identifying how malware operates, its propagation methods, and vulnerabilities it exploits. While this is a crucial part of cybersecurity, it often raises legal concerns.

Legal Challenges in Malware Analysis

1. **Software Copyright:** Malware is a form of software, and copyright laws may apply. Researchers must be cautious not to violate copyright laws when analyzing malware. They should focus on reverse engineering for security and not for unauthorized redistribution or replication.

2. **Unauthorized Access:** Malware samples are often distributed without the author's consent. Researchers should be mindful of the Computer Fraud and Abuse Act (CFAA) in the United States and similar laws in other jurisdictions. Unauthorized access to computer systems for analysis can have legal consequences.

3. **Data Privacy:** Malware analysis may involve the examination of data and files within the malware sample. Researchers must respect privacy laws and regulations, particularly when handling sensitive or personal data.

4. **Exemption for Security Research:** Some countries have exemptions in their copyright laws that allow for security research and malware analysis. For example, the DMCA in the United States provides certain exemptions for security research activities.

Best Practices for Legal Malware Analysis

1. **Obtain Legal Consent:** Whenever possible, obtain explicit consent or authorization from the owner of the system or software being analyzed. This can help protect researchers from potential legal issues.

2. **Use Controlled Environments:** Conduct malware analysis in controlled, isolated environments that do not affect other systems or networks. This minimizes the risk of unintended harm.

3. **Non-Malicious Intent:** Ensure that the intent of malware analysis is purely non-malicious. Researchers should not engage in activities that could be interpreted as hacking or cyberattacks.

4. **Responsible Disclosure:** If malware analysis identifies vulnerabilities or threats, follow responsible disclosure practices. Notify affected parties and collaborate on mitigations rather than exploiting the vulnerabilities for malicious purposes.

5. **Stay Informed:** Keep up-to-date with relevant cybersecurity laws, regulations, and guidelines in your jurisdiction and globally. Consult legal experts when necessary to ensure compliance.

Conclusion

Malware analysis is a vital component of cybersecurity, but it comes with legal responsibilities. Researchers and analysts must operate within the boundaries of the law and adhere to ethical guidelines. By obtaining legal consent, conducting analysis responsibly, and staying informed about legal developments, cybersecurity professionals can contribute to a safer digital environment.

Section 19.5: Privacy and Security in Assembly Development

Privacy and security are paramount concerns in assembly language development. This section explores the significance of privacy and security in assembly programming and provides guidelines to ensure code remains secure and respects user privacy.

The Importance of Privacy and Security

1. **Data Protection:** Assembly programs often deal with sensitive data. Protecting this data from unauthorized access or leaks is critical. Failure to do so can lead to data breaches and privacy violations.

2. **Malicious Exploitation:** Insecure assembly code can be exploited by attackers to gain unauthorized access, execute arbitrary code, or compromise system integrity. Security vulnerabilities can have severe consequences.

3. **Legal Compliance:** Many regions have strict data protection and privacy laws. Violating these laws can result in legal consequences, fines, and damage to an organization's reputation.

Privacy and Security Best Practices

1. **Secure Coding:** Follow secure coding practices to prevent common vulnerabilities like buffer overflows, injection attacks, and memory leaks. Utilize tools like static analyzers to identify security issues early in development.

2. **Data Encryption:** When handling sensitive data, employ encryption techniques to protect data both in transit and at rest. Utilize well-established encryption libraries and algorithms.

3. **Access Control:** Implement strict access control mechanisms to ensure that only authorized users or processes can interact with critical system components.

4. **Regular Updates:** Keep system components and libraries up-to-date. Security patches and updates should be applied promptly to address known vulnerabilities.

5. **User Authentication:** Implement robust user authentication mechanisms to verify the identity of users and prevent unauthorized access.

6. **Error Handling:** Proper error handling is essential. Avoid exposing sensitive information in error messages and logs. Instead, use generic error messages.

7. **Input Validation:** Validate and sanitize all user inputs to prevent injection attacks, such as SQL injection and cross-site scripting (XSS).

Privacy Considerations

1. **Data Minimization:** Collect only the data necessary for the program's functionality. Minimize data storage and retention to reduce the risk of data exposure.

2. **User Consent:** When collecting user data, obtain informed consent and make sure users are aware of how their data will be used.

3. **Anonymization:** If possible, anonymize or pseudonymize user data to protect identities while still achieving the program's objectives.

Compliance with Privacy Regulations

1. **GDPR (General Data Protection Regulation):** If your assembly program processes personal data of European Union residents, ensure compliance with GDPR, including data protection impact assessments, data subject rights, and breach notification requirements.

2. **HIPAA (Health Insurance Portability and Accountability Act):** If your assembly program handles healthcare information, adhere to HIPAA regulations regarding patient data privacy and security.

3. **CCPA (California Consumer Privacy Act):** If your assembly program collects personal information from California residents, comply with CCPA requirements, including data access and deletion requests.

Conclusion

Privacy and security should be integral to every aspect of assembly language development. By following best practices, staying informed about relevant privacy regulations, and prioritizing secure coding, developers can create assembly programs that protect user data and systems from potential threats and vulnerabilities.

Chapter 20: Future Trends in Assembly Programming

Section 20.1: Evolving ISAs and Architectures

In the ever-changing landscape of technology, assembly language programming continues to adapt and evolve. This section delves into the future trends of assembly programming, focusing on the evolution of Instruction Set Architectures (ISAs) and computer architectures.

The Role of ISAs in Evolution

Instruction Set Architectures (ISAs) serve as the foundation for programming languages and software development. The future of assembly programming is closely intertwined with how ISAs evolve:

1. **RISC-V Revolution:** The RISC-V (Reduced Instruction Set Computer - V) architecture has gained momentum as an open-source ISA. Its extensibility and adaptability make it attractive for various applications, including embedded systems and high-performance computing.

2. **Specialized ISAs:** As workloads become more specialized, we may witness the rise of specialized ISAs tailored for specific tasks. For example, machine learning or quantum computing may have dedicated ISAs optimized for their unique requirements.

3. **Quantum Assembly:** Quantum computing is emerging as a new frontier. Programming quantum computers requires a fundamentally different approach, and quantum assembly languages are being developed to harness the power of quantum processors.

Architectural Trends

Architectural changes also shape the future of assembly programming:

1. **Heterogeneous Computing:** Modern systems often integrate CPUs, GPUs, TPUs, and other accelerators. Assembly programmers will need to work with heterogeneous architectures efficiently, utilizing each component's strengths.

2. **Quantum Architectures:** As quantum computers become more practical, assembly programming for quantum processors will be a specialized skill. Quantum architectures are fundamentally different, and developers will need to adapt to this new paradigm.

3. **Neuromorphic Computing:** Neuromorphic chips, designed to mimic the human brain's architecture, may introduce new assembly programming challenges and opportunities in areas like AI and cognitive computing.

With evolving ISAs and architectures, new programming abstractions may arise:

1. **High-Level Assembly:** High-level assembly languages may bridge the gap between low-level assembly and high-level languages, providing better abstractions for complex tasks while maintaining performance.

2. **AI-Assisted Programming:** AI and machine learning may assist assembly programmers in optimizing code and identifying potential vulnerabilities.

3. **Domain-Specific Languages (DSLs):** DSLs tailored for specific industries or applications may simplify assembly programming in specialized domains.

Challenges and Opportunities

The future of assembly programming offers both challenges and opportunities:

1. **Performance and Power Efficiency:** Meeting the growing demand for performance while maintaining power efficiency will be a perpetual challenge.

2. **Security:** As systems become more interconnected, assembly programmers will play a crucial role in ensuring the security of critical infrastructure and applications.

3. **Education and Skills:** Teaching assembly programming and keeping developers skilled in this domain will be vital for the industry's growth.

4. **Innovation:** Assembly programmers will continue to innovate in areas such as quantum computing, AI, and IoT, driving technological advancements.

In conclusion, the future of assembly programming is marked by the evolution of ISAs, diverse architectures, and the emergence of new programming abstractions. While challenges exist, assembly language remains a fundamental skill for those who seek to understand and shape the future of computing. Adapting to these trends will ensure that assembly programming remains relevant and influential in the years to come.

Section 20.2: Quantum Assembly's Potential

Quantum computing represents one of the most exciting and disruptive technologies on the horizon, and quantum assembly language is at the heart of programming these quantum machines. In this section, we explore the potential and challenges of quantum assembly.

Quantum Computing Fundamentals

Quantum computing harnesses the principles of quantum mechanics to perform calculations that are practically impossible for classical computers. Instead of classical bits, quantum computers use quantum bits or qubits. Quantum states like superposition and entanglement enable quantum computers to process vast amounts of information simultaneously.

Quantum assembly languages, such as QASM (Quantum Assembly Language) for IBM's Qiskit and Quipper for Microsoft's Q# language, provide a low-level interface to program quantum computers. These languages allow developers to define quantum circuits, gates, and operations.

```
qreg q[2];   // Define a quantum register with 2 qubits
creg c[2];   // Define a classical register with 2 bits

// Apply a Hadamard gate to the first qubit
h q[0];

// Apply a CNOT gate (controlled-X) between the qubits
cx q[0], q[1];

// Measure the qubits and store the results in classical bits
measure q -> c;
```

Quantum Assembly vs. Classical Assembly

Quantum assembly programming differs significantly from classical assembly. While classical assembly manipulates bits and performs logical and arithmetic operations, quantum assembly deals with qubits and quantum gates. Quantum gates can operate on multiple qubits simultaneously, leading to complex quantum algorithms.

Quantum Algorithms and Applications

Quantum assembly's potential lies in its ability to solve problems that are infeasible for classical computers:

1. **Factorization:** Quantum computers can efficiently factor large numbers, posing a threat to classical encryption methods like RSA.

2. **Optimization:** Quantum algorithms can optimize complex systems, such as financial portfolios or supply chains, more quickly than classical methods.

3. **Drug Discovery:** Quantum computing accelerates drug discovery by simulating molecular interactions with high precision.

4. **Machine Learning:** Quantum machine learning algorithms promise exponential speedup for certain tasks.

5. **Quantum Simulation:** Simulating quantum systems, such as the behavior of molecules, materials, and particles, is a natural fit for quantum computers.

Despite its potential, quantum assembly faces several challenges:

1. **Hardware Constraints:** Practical quantum computers are still in their infancy, and they suffer from errors, limited qubit counts, and short coherence times. Quantum assembly programmers must account for these constraints.

2. **Algorithm Development:** Designing quantum algorithms and expressing them in quantum assembly requires expertise in both quantum physics and programming.

3. **Education and Training:** A shortage of skilled quantum programmers is an industry-wide concern. Education and training programs are needed to prepare developers for this emerging field.

4. **Quantum Error Correction:** Developing effective error correction codes is crucial to making quantum computing reliable and practical.

In conclusion, quantum assembly language represents a frontier of computing, offering the potential to revolutionize industries and scientific research. However, it's a field of study that requires a deep understanding of quantum physics and a willingness to embrace the challenges of a rapidly evolving technology. As quantum hardware matures and quantum programming tools improve, quantum assembly will play a pivotal role in unlocking the full power of quantum computing.

Section 20.3: Assembly in the Age of AI

As we step into an era defined by artificial intelligence (AI) and machine learning (ML), the role of assembly language in computing continues to evolve. In this section, we'll explore how assembly language is adapting to and intersecting with the domains of AI and ML.

Assembly Language's Historical Relevance

Assembly language has a rich history of low-level programming, dating back to the early days of computing. It was instrumental in writing the first compilers, operating systems, and software tools that laid the foundation for modern computing. As we embrace AI and ML, assembly retains its relevance, but in new and exciting ways.

AI and ML Hardware Acceleration

AI and ML rely heavily on matrix operations, which involve large datasets and complex mathematical computations. To speed up these operations, specialized hardware, such as graphics processing units (GPUs) and tensor processing units (TPUs), have become essential. Assembly language plays a crucial role in optimizing code for these hardware accelerators.

```
; Example assembly code for matrix multiplication on a GPU
matrix_mult:
```

```
    mov r0, a        ; Load matrix A into register r0
    mov r1, b        ; Load matrix B into register r1
    mov r2, result   ; Load result matrix address into r2

    ...
    ; Matrix multiplication algorithm
    ...
    ret
```

Low-Level Optimization

AI and ML libraries often use high-level languages like Python or R for ease of development. However, for performance-critical components, assembly language can be used to optimize specific functions or algorithms. This fine-grained optimization can lead to significant speed improvements.

```
// C code
double dot_product(double* a, double* b, int size) {
    double result = 0.0;
    for (int i = 0; i < size; i++) {
        result += a[i] * b[i];
    }
    return result;
}
```

```
; Assembly code for optimized dot product
dot_product:
    xorpd xmm0, xmm0        ; Clear xmm0 register
    xor r8d, r8d            ; Clear r8 register
    xor r9d, r9d            ; Clear r9 register
.loop:
    movsd xmm1, [rdi+r8]    ; Load a[i] into xmm1
    movsd xmm2, [rsi+r8]    ; Load b[i] into xmm2
    mulsd xmm1, xmm2        ; Multiply a[i] by b[i]
    addsd xmm0, xmm1        ; Add the result to xmm0
    add r8, 8               ; Increment loop counter
    cmp r8, rcx             ; Compare with size
    jl .loop                ; Jump if less
    ret
```

Real-Time AI and IoT

In the context of the Internet of Things (IoT) and real-time AI applications, assembly language becomes valuable due to its deterministic nature and ability to control hardware directly. For instance, assembly can be used to implement sensor data processing algorithms or manage real-time AI inference on resource-constrained devices.

AI and ML Frameworks with Assembly Support

Some AI and ML frameworks provide assembly-level interfaces for performance-critical operations. For example, Intel's oneDNN (formerly known as MKL-DNN) library allows developers to leverage low-level optimizations using assembly language for deep learning operations.

In conclusion, assembly language continues to play a vital role in the age of AI and ML. While high-level languages dominate AI development, assembly's low-level optimization capabilities make it a valuable tool for accelerating critical components. Whether it's optimizing code for specialized hardware or enabling real-time AI on IoT devices, assembly language remains a powerful asset in the AI and ML toolbox.

Section 20.4: Assembly and IoT Integration

The integration of assembly language and the Internet of Things (IoT) represents a fascinating synergy of low-level programming and embedded systems. In this section, we'll explore how assembly language is applied in the context of IoT, enabling efficient and resource-conscious development for a wide range of connected devices.

The IoT Landscape

IoT encompasses a diverse array of devices, from tiny sensors to industrial equipment, all connected to the internet. These devices collect data, make decisions, and interact with their environments. To achieve this, they often have limited computational resources, power constraints, and specialized hardware.

Low-Level Control

Assembly language's role in IoT development becomes evident when considering the need for precise control over hardware components. IoT devices often require direct management of sensors, actuators, and communication interfaces. Assembly provides the ability to write firmware that interacts efficiently with this hardware.

```
; Example assembly code for reading sensor data
read_sensor_data:
    mov r0, sensor_address
    mov r1, data_buffer
    ; Perform sensor data reading and storing
    ...
    ret
```

Energy Efficiency

IoT devices are often battery-powered or have stringent power requirements. Assembly's fine-grained control over hardware can be leveraged to optimize power consumption. This includes techniques like putting components to sleep when not in use and managing power states efficiently.

Real-Time Processing

Some IoT applications, such as industrial control systems and autonomous vehicles, demand real-time responsiveness. Assembly's deterministic nature allows developers to meet strict timing requirements, ensuring reliable and predictable operation.

```
; Example assembly code for real-time control
real_time_control:
    mov r0, control_parameters
    ; Perform real-time control operations
    ...
    ret
```

Resource-Conscious Development

IoT devices often have limited memory and storage. Assembly's ability to write highly compact code is advantageous in such scenarios, helping minimize the footprint of firmware and reducing costs associated with memory and storage.

IoT Protocols and Communication

Assembly can be employed to implement communication protocols used in IoT, such as MQTT, CoAP, or LoRaWAN. These protocols require efficient data encoding, encryption, and transmission, which assembly's low-level capabilities can address.

```
; Example assembly code for MQTT packet encoding
encode_mqtt_packet:
    mov r0, message_data
    mov r1, encoded_packet
    ; Perform MQTT packet encoding
    ...
    ret
```

IoT Security

Security is paramount in IoT, especially when devices are deployed in critical applications or are part of large-scale networks. Assembly's role extends to implementing security measures, including encryption, authentication, and access control, to safeguard IoT ecosystems.

In conclusion, assembly language is an indispensable tool in the IoT landscape, offering precise control, energy efficiency, real-time capabilities, resource-conscious development, and the means to address security challenges. As IoT continues to grow and diversify, assembly's relevance in enabling efficient and reliable device operation remains unwavering.

Section 20.5: The Continued Relevance of Assembly Language

Despite the evolution of programming languages and the rise of high-level abstractions, assembly language remains relevant in several domains. In this section, we'll explore why assembly language continues to have a place in modern computing.

Legacy Systems and Maintenance

One of the primary reasons for the continued use of assembly language is its relevance in maintaining and extending legacy systems. Many critical software components, such as device drivers and embedded firmware, are originally written in assembly. Developers often need to modify or update these components, making assembly knowledge essential.

```
; Example assembly code for a legacy device driver
legacy_driver:
    mov r0, device_parameters
    ; Perform device control operations
    ...
    ret
```

Real-Time Systems

Assembly language excels in real-time systems, where precise timing and low-level hardware control are essential. Applications like robotics, industrial automation, and aerospace systems rely on assembly to meet stringent timing requirements and ensure safe and predictable operation.

Embedded Systems

Embedded systems, powering everything from consumer electronics to automotive control units, rely heavily on assembly. Its ability to produce compact and efficient code makes it suitable for resource-constrained microcontrollers and processors commonly used in embedded applications.

Kernel and Operating System Development

Kernel development and operating system internals often involve assembly programming. Writing parts of the kernel or handling interrupt routines requires low-level control over hardware, which assembly provides. Even in modern operating systems, certain critical sections are implemented in assembly for performance reasons.

```
; Example assembly code for an interrupt handler
interrupt_handler:
    ; Handle hardware interrupt
    ...
    reti
```

Reverse Engineering and Security

In the fields of reverse engineering and cybersecurity, assembly language plays a crucial role. Security analysts and penetration testers use assembly to analyze and understand the behavior of binary executables, identify vulnerabilities, and develop exploits.

```
; Example assembly code for a security exploit
security_exploit:
    ; Exploit a vulnerability
    ...
    ret
```

Optimization and Performance Tuning

When squeezing the last bit of performance from hardware is essential, assembly language shines. High-performance computing, scientific simulations, and multimedia processing often leverage assembly for hand-optimized routines that outperform their high-level language counterparts.

Teaching and Learning

Assembly language is frequently used in computer science and computer engineering education. It provides students with a deep understanding of computer architecture, memory management, and low-level programming concepts, laying the foundation for advanced studies in these fields.

Conclusion

While high-level languages have simplified software development and made it more accessible, assembly language remains an indispensable tool for tasks requiring fine-grained control, optimization, and interfacing with hardware. Its unique strengths ensure that it will continue to have a place in various domains of computing for the foreseeable future. As technology continues to advance, assembly language programmers will play a vital role in bridging the gap between hardware and software.

www.ingramcontent.com/pod-product-compliance
Lightning Source LLC
Chambersburg PA
CBHW071246050326
40690CB00011B/2286